The Simple Guide to Feeling Better

Susan D. Kalior, M.A. in Counseling/Human
Relations and Behavior, B.S. Sociology

The Simple Guide to Feeling Better

Copyright ©2016 by Susan D Kalior
Published by Blue Wing Publications, Workshops, and Lectures

First Printing : June 2016
ISBN 978-0692739426

sdk@bluewingworkshops.com
www.bluewingworkshops.com
Readers comments are welcomed. Remember to leave a review!
Join mailing list for future updates at: http://eepurl.com/b2Ymo5

Manufactured in the United States of America

Other Books by Susan D. Kalior

Growing Wings Self-Discovery Workbook:
   17 Workshops to a Better Life-Volume One
Growing Wings Self-Discovery Workbook:
   18 Workshops to a Better Life Volume Two
The Other Side of God: The Eleven Gem Odyssey of Being
The Other Side of Life: The Eleven Gem Odyssey of Death
The Mark of Chaos
An Angel's Touch
The Golden Disc
Warriors in the Mist: A Dark Fantasy
The Dark Side of Light: A Time Travel Fantasy

Dedication

To everyone, everywhere, doing the best they can.

Table of Contents

Introduction

We all suffer in varying degrees at times in our lives. Our suffering is mostly due to life circumstance, loss, or other people's behavior toward us. While deeper probing into our psyche with a therapist or plunging ourselves into the depths of self-discovery can yield greater self-understanding and significant life change, this simple guide offers immediate solutions that do not require change in the people around us, or our life circumstance. Even so, these easy techniques most often result in a productive change in both.

The Basics

1
CALM DOWN

Breathe. Just breathe, slowly, steadily, and deeply. When upset, our breathing is either exceedingly rapid, slow and shallow, or barely at all.

When distressed, inhale relief through your nose, by slowly and simultaneously ballooning your abdomen and filling your chest with air to capacity. Then, in a soothing exhalation from your mouth, slowly and simultaneously contract your abdomen and expel all air from your lungs. Repeat until calm.

The first step to calming down
is to breathe s l o w l y, steadily, and deeply.

Our emotions affect our breathing, and our breathing affects our emotions. No matter what the upset, slow, deep, steady breathing calms us. It is virtually impossible to maintain our level of distress when breathing this way. With this technique, we can begin to take charge of our stressful emotions.

While calming down does not solve our problems, it increases our chances of solving them with stellar results. Panic, and/or feeling beaten are the top reasons people falter. These urges can be powerful. Yet, panic frequently begets tragedy, and giving up is tantamount to defeat.

1

Actions taken when stressed differ from actions taken when calm.

When we calm down, we:

*think more clearly

*act rationally

*do not overreact and make everything worse

*are less likely to take our frustrations out on others

*change tragic outlooks to brighter outcomes

When stressed, practice self-control.

While there is always a time for anger to spur us into action, sorrow to grieve our loss, or fear to keep us safe, these emotions when uncontrolled, can hijack reason and make our lives worse. Calming down can help us harness our emotions to navigate our lives in a more productive manner.

The first thing we are told when getting caught in an ocean rip current is don't panic. Those who don't make it usually panic and eventually give up. Those who survive, calmly and persistently swim parallel to the shore. This occurrence holds true for all stressful situations. When we remain calm and productively focused, we improve our chances of coming out on top.

If we follow a few simple rules, we can not only succeed in calming down, but remain calm with relative ease.

1. *Regulate breathing.* As just discussed, when stressed, breathe slowly, deeply, and steadily. Think, *Everything will go better if I remain calm.*

2. *Focus on the desired finish line.* Our thoughts often jump to the worst conclusion possible. We form doom and gloom assumptions that influence our actions. If instead, we keep our focus on the finish line, such as seeing ourselves home safe, being debt free, or enjoying our lives again after a great loss, our current fears begin to fade as our focus is now upon a desirable

end game. This gives us positive direction while inhibiting our minds from spinning destructive thoughts. This is not about trying to will the future we want into existence, but rather remaining calm enough to give that future a *chance* to happen.

3. *Refrain from snap decisions.* Let a day or two pass before making any rash decision. We humans can get sucked into the excitement of the moment as well as the fear of 'act now or else'. Con artists count on us to succumb to this pitch. While not everyone who makes such a pitch is a con artist, these snap decisions are often not in our best interest.

Even one night's sleep and a day of pondering can help us see the bigger picture and the possible consequences of moving ahead with any given decision. We might ultimately make that decision, but it will be made with forethought and diminishing the chances of backfire.

4. *Take things in stride.* Sometimes it feels like an unsavory future is inevitable based on our past experience and current predicament. However, this imagined future is merely speculation based on our present point of view. Even our remembered past is based on the point of view we had *then*.

Our viewpoints change as we move along in life; hence, whatever seems true at the moment, may not be true in our future. Around the corner from any seeming disaster, there is another view. We just haven't got there yet.

So as we sit in our present, if we take things in stride instead of trying to rush a result, we not only prevent destructive outcomes but we ensure our own evolvement by just allowing the process to take us there. Just as a baby needs time to develop in the womb, we too need time to develop throughout the course of our lives.

When we are patient and compassionate with ourselves, time will bring us along all on its own. Then one day, like the seedling breaking ground, we will emerge into the light, and the next step of our evolution. Like the caterpillar encased in a seeming eternity of darkness, we too are all destined to fly.

Life is in a constant state of change.
and so are we.

Everything happens in its own time. We cannot rush our life story. We can only take it as it comes, and extract some joy along the way.

Points to Remember

1. When we calm our breathing, we calm our emotions.

2. Focus on the desired finish line, not our fears.

3. Avoid snap decisions that can work against us.

4. Take things in stride instead of trying to rush a result.

2
KNOW YOUR WORTH

Our self-worth is under constant scrutiny by the social world, our significant others, and ourselves, as if our worth *is* what other people say it is.

This could not be farther from the truth. Our ideas of self-worth are based solely on *opinions*, not fact. Given the billions of people on earth, opinions can vary dramatically. In that, the idea that one's worth is what someone says it is, doesn't even make sense. A person's worth cannot be measured by opinions. In fact, it can't be measured at all.

Just like every flower in the meadow, bird in the sky, and child on earth, our worth is invaluable, intrinsic, and forever. We are born with it and we die with it. It cannot be given or taken. Our worth has nothing to do with achievement, how we look, our age, or how much money we make. Our worth has nothing do with who does or does not love us, or who does and does not approve of us. Even if we don't love ourselves, our worth does not diminish. No matter what we say or do, or what is said or done to us, our worth does not go up or down, and it is equal to everything else in existence.

Our self-worth is intrinsic,
invaluable, and forever.

When we know our worth, we:

   *are not shaken by other people's opinions of us

   *can heal from past trauma

   *can admit if we were wrong

*are kinder to everyone

*improve our life direction

*love ourselves no matter what

*act from self worth, not for self worth

*do our part to change the world

Overcoming Social Programming

Unlike other forms of life, we have a rather extensive intellect. We draw conclusions and react to what we *decide* to believe, for example, *My mom keeps criticizing me, therefore I am no good.*

The struggle to uphold our value is compounded by our high tech mass media bombarding us with messages that we must achieve certain criteria if we are to be deemed worthy, such as a particular physical image, or monetary status.

The quest to achieve these criteria can chip away at our self-esteem, and incite anxiety. The message is that who we are matters less than what others say we *should* be. Self-judgment abounds as we ever strive to measure up, feeling less worthy if we fall short.

Yet, these criteria are just what people have made up and agreed upon, be they familial, community, or societal. These *opinions* in no way govern our self-worth.

The solution to feeling always valued is to *never* devalue ourselves. In this, we harness great personal power. In valuing ourselves as we would the stars or a newborn baby, we quite literally cannot be emotionally hurt (or at least for long), or derailed from feeling good. We acknowledge our self-worth from within, and no amount of social programming can hijack it.

Healing from Past Trauma

Our sense of worth is further tested if we are chronically insulted, assaulted, or criticized. This bombardment over time can erode our self-esteem and cause psychological wounds.

These wounds stay with us even if we pretend they are not there. Because life is life, we all have psychological wounds in varying degrees, evident when we are unreasonably set off by particular words or actions from others.

If we have been called lazy all our lives, when really we had *Attention Deficit Disorder*, giving us a focus problem, we might feel rage toward anyone who calls us lazy, and spew a hostile defense.

If we were raised to value a clean home over emotional well-being, an insinuation that there is any imperfection in our home might trigger an all night cleaning frenzy at the expense of sleep, food, and even kindness toward others.

When our soft spots are poked, we feel our self-worth is in question, and we are more likely to overreact. We might want to retaliate, or engage others to side with us, or feel like it is the end of the world, or at least our world, making us question if life is worth living. Often, the actual event that unleashed all this emotion is quite trivial. We just have a truckload of pain attached to similar past events that made us feel unworthy. Hence, the trivial event feels monstrous.

When we begin to separate our worth from our experiences, we initiate healing. Here are some examples: *I got rejected, but I still measure up. I was treated poorly, but I am a valuable person in my own right. I am important, no matter what . . . no . . . matter . . . what.* The more healed we are, the less reactive we will be when poked in those sensitive areas.

Overcoming Regret

Sometimes what keeps us from feeling good about ourselves are our regrets. Regrets are nothing more than things we did that *at that time* seemed to be alright. In hindsight, we can see the consequences of our choices. If we had known in advance where those choices would have led us, we likely would have chosen differently. We *all* have done things we regret because none of us has one hundred percent foresight all the time. We have always done our best for, who we were, what we knew, and the stresses we endured *then*. Now is now. Then was then. Do we shame the walking child for once crawling?

Overcoming regret is easier when we follow two simple rules:

1. *Turn regrets into lessons learned*. When we can change for the better based on what we did in the past, then good can come from it. For example, if we treated someone harshly when he or she didn't deserve it, we can strive to behave differently in the future.

2. *Be compassionate with ourselves*. When we feel guilty about our past actions, we often forget the stresses we were under at that time that facilitated our behavior. We only focus on what went wrong. Even if there were better ways we could have handled something, at *that time*, we just couldn't. By being compassionate with ourselves, we will also remember what we did right, which in fact, will overwhelmingly outweigh our blunders.

Mistakes do not demean our worth.

The word mistake generally has a negative connotation. However, mistakes are just choices we make that don't turn out so well. We are not less worthy for making mistakes or experiencing so-called failure. Even animals and plants will make adjustments to survive and thrive. Sometimes it doesn't turn out so well. If a seal swims into a shark's path and gets eaten, it doesn't mean it is less worthy than another seal. And sometimes the mistake of one is the fortune of another. For instance, the seal who swam into the shark's path has given the shark food to live another day.

We are all worthy despite our state of being.

Some flowers might be healthy, others drooping. Some people are emaciated and others plump. Some oceans are clean and others polluted. However, every flower, ocean, and person is equal in worth. They only differ in their *state of being*. Our state of being does not reflect our value, just as a person with a missing limb is no less valuable than a person with all limbs intact. The mentally healthy person is not more valuable than the psychologically tormented person. And so it goes that the bum on the street is no less valuable than the well-dressed millionaire.

We are always invaluable
despite our state of being.

Often banged, bruised, and worse for the wear, we carry on the best we can. We are not supposed to know how to perfectly navigate ourselves through the maze of life, for the path is different for everyone. At times we will bump into walls, feel frustration, despaired, or become lost along the way. Sometimes we behave in varying degrees of dishonor out of fear or a dire attempt to feel better. None of us need be admonished for trying to make it through the day.

We simply learn by trial and error, what works and what doesn't. If we get kicked in the teeth, it doesn't mean we aren't worthy. If we kick others in the teeth, it doesn't mean that they aren't worthy. This doesn't mean we or others do not take consequences for our actions. We do, do we ever, but we are always worthy!

Natural consequences are not punishment.

We never get away with anything, for life is a great teacher. Natural consequences catch up with us one way or another. We break the law; we go to jail. We cheat others long enough, we wind up alone and lonely. We give ourselves away, and we get used. We respect ourselves, and we are respected. We love ourselves, and it easier to love others.

These consequences are not our punishment, but just the result of what happens when we do this or that. You eat, you get fed. You don't eat, you starve.

While consequences are inherent in our folly, our worth is never in question. *What we do* might be in question, but not our worth.

No matter what we do, we are always worthy.

It's okay to be wrong.

Sometimes we feel our self-worth will be compromised if we admit we are wrong. Being right makes us feel powerful and in control, so we insist we are right, even if we aren't.

Being wrong doesn't mean we are bad or unworthy. It means we are secure enough to look at ourselves and improve our inadequacies. Interestingly, people seem to love us more when we take responsibility for our folly.

Act from self-worth, not for self-worth.

When our actions are motivated to enhance self-worth, which is perfectly normal, so that we can feel better about ourselves, the pressure is on. We must succeed in order to like ourselves. If self-worth is at stake, a sense of desperation prevails, and we fear failing.

When this happens, we would fair better to shift our thinking slightly from, *If I do this I will be more worthy*, to *I am worth taking steps to improve my life.* When we know our worth, mountains of stress are lifted off our shoulders. If our self-worth is not at stake, then the need to achieve comes from a place of self-love, enthusiasm, and joy.

The same principle applies to our often all-consuming quest to be valued by others. If we get it, we feel good. If we don't, we feel bad. Either way, we are giving others power over our feelings and making our worth conditional. They get to decide if we will feel good or not.

The irony is that what we want from others almost always comes to us naturally, when first we give it to ourselves.

When we affirm our worth, we emanate confidence, charisma, and we shine. This is what makes us look beautiful, much more than enhancing our physical appeal. Shining our inner beauty attracts positive people and events into our lives.

Let your motto be: *I am invaluable, always.*

When we begin to believe this, we naturally shine our authentic selves into the world. This opens doors and allows us to grow into our full potential, despite *anything* that happens to us.

Acting from self-worth instead of for self-worth can be achieved by following three simple rules:

1. *Resist the urge to gain approval.* Take a deep breath and say, "I am already worthy. I don't need anyone's approval."

2. *Focus on fostering personal growth.* Ask, "How can I improve my life?"

3. *Appreciate your unique gifts, and celebrate the meaningful things you have already done.* Say, "Just by being myself, I have made and will continue to make a positive mark in this world."

Make the world a better place.

When we feel unworthy, our actions create a negative ripple of insecurity out into the world, that over the course of a lifetime, will negatively affect thousands, maybe more. When we know our worth is invaluable, our actions send out a positive ripple that will echo out into future generations. The ripple carries forth the message: *Embrace your worth no matter what happened to you, or what you have done. Embrace it deep with pure heart, and don't look back.* If enough people did this, it would change the world.

So, every time we behold our worth invaluable *as is*, we are also doing our part to make the world a better place.

Points to Remember

1. Self-worth is intrinsic and not measured by opinions.

2. We are all worthy, despite our actions.

3. Learn from past actions to improve our present.

4. We all make mistakes, and learn by trial and error.

5. People like us more if we can admit when we are wrong.

6. Natural consequences are inevitable for all.

7. Natural consequences are not punishment.

8. Act from self-worth, not for self-worth.

9. When we know our worth, we better the world.

3
THINK PRODUCTIVELY

Just as we program a computer, we program ourselves. What we say to ourselves, does matter. In short, as we think, so shall we experience.

Thinking productively, such as *I'll do better next time,* we feel better. Thinking negatively, such as *I ruined everything,* we feel worse.

When we think productively, we:

*control our reality

*relieve inner turmoil

*dis-invite trauma

*have a meaningful life, despite what occurs

*enable ourselves to live to the fullest

*make a beneficial mark in our corner of the world

Productive thinking is not the same as positive thinking.

Productive thinking, which is not the same as positive thinking, can completely change our lives. While productive thinking is positive thinking, not all a positive thinking is productive.

Positive thinking, such as *I can do this; I will be okay,* is very powerful. We are feeding a belief in *ourselves* to get the job done. However, when positive thinking involves assuming the best will happen, for example, *The relationship will all work out, or I am sure I'll get the job,* we are feeding a belief that *others* will comply to our wishes. This kind of positive thinking is a way of kidding ourselves into staying calm. This definitely has merit, and works with somewhat mixed results, however, productive thinking never, never fails.

Positive thinking is also used as a method to attempt manifesting our wishes, for example, *I will be chosen for that job* and visualizing all other competitors falling out of the employers mind. Or, *I will make him love me. I can do it.*

While this effort can definitely contribute to the desired outcome, it often doesn't because *others* have their own free will and their desired outcome might counter ours. When our positive thinking fails to deliver, we are often left feeling disappointed, mostly in ourselves, deeming we have failed.

If, on the other hand, the desired result is achieved, these forced results are not necessarily productive. We don't always know what is best for us, even if we think we do. Manipulating our way into that job may not actually be the best job for us. Around the corner might be a better match. Forcing (manipulating) a person to love us is only short-lived because everyone is who they are, and everything is what it is. We can manipulate it, but the force of nature is strong, and will eventually right itself to *what is.* Then, our positive thinking, which was an effort to force our will to be actualized, was just a diversion from our own natural evolvement.

Examples of *productive thinking* in these two instances would be:

I will do my best to get the job; if it doesn't work out, then it wasn't the job for me. I will be okay no matter what.

I will be my true self, and I will be okay whether she loves me back or not. If she doesn't, she isn't the mate for me, and I deserve the right match

In both circumstances, there is NO losing. You are a winner no

.

matter what happens. By thinking productively, we can take our lives in a more fulfilling direction despite the challenges we encounter, or the fearful thoughts running through our brain.

The Dynamics of Productive Thinking

Dynamic 1. Our thoughts dictate our mood.

Dynamic 2. Our mood influences our actions.

Dynamic 3. Our actions create our reality.

Dynamic 4. Our reality is maintained by what we spotlight.

It all starts with a thought.

Given our mood, actions, and reality are influenced by our initial thoughts, it is important to realize that our thoughts *are merely opinions* or *assumptions*, and not necessarily true. Our whole day can be affected by one thought.

Example:

Oh no, the acceptance letter I was waiting for still hasn't come! I must have been rejected. What am I going to do now? This is going to be a rotten day. We get grumpy, wanting the day to be over. We tense up waiting for the next bad thing to happen. We move about our day with a sad face or glaring eye, and others respond to us in kind. We are not at our best, so we miss important clues to avoid mistakes, and don't see the good things right in front of us. This all results in a rotten day. It might even be that the letter comes later, having originally been mailed to the wrong address. Then all that upset was unnecessary.

If instead, given the above example, we think like this:

Well, maybe I got rejected and maybe I didn't. Either way, I can handle it. If it comes, great. If not, I can always come up with a plan B. (Not, *oh I am sure the letter just got delayed, but it's coming*). Feeling confident in ourselves, we walk about with a bounce in our step and a smile on our face, and unsavory would be events are short-circuited by our self-reliance, kindness, and joy. If we should be met by a challenge, knowing we can handle it, we are empowered. By days end, we feel pretty good about ourselves.

However, more commonly, we humans tend to assume our conclusions are the truth, and act upon them. The news is filled with stories of those who acted on assumption, creating gruesome realities. Here are some examples: *My lover did me wrong. She will pay!* (It could be that the lover canceled a date due to feeling unwell, and that was construed as cheating.) Or, *He did that on purpose just to get back at me. Now I will get back at him.* It could be that "he" doesn't even know what you are talking about.

When we find ourselves thinking darkly, we can feel better by doing three things:

1. *Open your mind.* Pry open your mind just a crack with this productive thought: *Just because I am thinking this, doesn't make it true.* It is a good rule of thumb to not unequivocally believe what you think, but acknowledge it is just one *perception* based on how you feel at the moment. This alone can stop us from acting on imagined truths or misinterpretations of what we have seen or heard.

2. *Believe in yourself.* Tell yourself, "Even if it is true, I can handle it. I can take charge of my life and make it a good one, no matter what happens to me."

3. *Do something positive for yourself.* Ask yourself, "What kind thing can I do for myself?" Examples: listen to beautiful music, go out in nature, paint a picture, watch a show, sign up for a class, get a therapist, or just cry and feel compassion for yourself. By changing your dark thinking channel to a productive one, we can let in the light to save the day.

Pay attention to repetitive thoughts.

Repetitive thoughts become our beliefs.

We might bombard ourselves with self-defeating lines such as: *I don't matter. I don't measure up. There is no hope for me. Nobody cares about me. Everyone has it better than me. It's not fair.* Eventually, we believe it. These depressive beliefs often lead to deep sadness, destructive anger, and mental breakdown.

We might tell ourselves repeatedly: *I matter. I am always valuable. I can take charge of my life. I am growing into my true self.* Eventually, we come to believe it.

These beliefs, whatever they are, dictate our behavior. Our beliefs steer our lives. If we don't like where we are going, dismantle the beliefs that are driving us in that direction. We do this by stopping the repetitive thoughts that keep them active and instead insert new, more productive lines of thought.

Replace negative thoughts with productive thoughts.

The moment you feel bad, take note of what you are thinking. It will likely be something unsavory. Then, replace those thoughts with productive ones.

For example, be aware of thoughts such as these: *I am trying so hard and I can't seem to get ahead. I'll never make it. I am a failure. I don't have what it takes. I'm bad. I am unworthy. No one appreciates me. Everyone is better than me. I am weak and inferior. I always get cheated. There is no hope, why even try?*

Then replace them with productive thoughts, such as these: *I am doing the best I can. I appreciate what is good in me. I will celebrate my strengths, and my uniqueness. I am strong and smart. I can handle anything that comes my way. I can still enjoy the stars, and the sweet things of life. I am valuable no matter what. My effort shows my good will. The way I treat others is worth more than getting ahead. I really appreciate myself. I am going to enjoy my day; I deserve that.*

When we give ourselves half a chance by learning to think productively, we can significantly enrich our reality. Best of all, we learn we can depend upon ourselves, not only to survive, but to flourish into all we can be.

Spotlighting

Spotlighting is focusing on specific areas of our lives that take on more meaning than the rest. Wherever our mind lingers most becomes our priority.

The spotlight might be a goal: making money, losing weight, writing that book. Or it might be psychological: getting approval, generating sympathy, or controlling others.

Sometimes we spotlight a theme, such as *perceiving* how unfairly we are treated, winning all the time, or striving to be perfect.

Wherever our spotlight is, be it positive or negative, that is the direction we will go.

Spotlighting *can* be helpful if it improves our lives. For example, in spotlighting the simple things that bring us joy, we can feel better instantly. Spotlighting a relationship we wish to improve, can result in a very meaningful experience. If we spotlight being kinder to ourselves or taking charge of our lives, we can feel ourselves flourishing.

Negative spotlights such as jealousy, revenge, low self-esteem, or feeling chronically victimized, erode our well-being. Spotlighting can also be destructive if we make it our whole world to the exclusion of other areas of our lives.

Negative spotlighting erodes our well-being.

If we are an artist and work on our piece for forty days and forty nights forgetting to eat, barely sleeping, shooing away our loved ones, and forget to pay the bills, this is not so good for our health or anyone else in our life. Granted the creative process often requires intense prolonged concentration, however, any obsession, including obsession with a person, can literally drive us mad.

If our spotlight is fixated on feeling cheated, we will view everything through that lens and be consumed by that reality.

If our spotlight is on always being right, we will bite off our nose to spite our face. We might dominate every argument, but our relationships are in shambles.

We can abolish damaging spotlighting with productive thinking in the following ways:

If spotlighting a need for approval, think, *I approve of myself.*

If spotlighting poor self-image, think, *I am invaluable always.*

If spotlighting a need to control someone, think, *I have control over myself. I don't need to control others.*

If spotlighting depression, think, *I can take charge of my own reality.*

If spotlighting money issues, think, *There are more important things in life, such as kindness and love.*

If spotlighting feeling used and abused, think, *I respect myself so I am going to change this situation.*

If spotlighting feeling unappreciated, think, *I appreciate myself. I'm going to treat myself better.*

In all cases, it can be helpful if we learn to move our spotlight around to see what is going on in other areas of our lives, such as our children, our friends, our home, our health, our deep down needs, and what is going on inside us. To be a well-rounded person, learn to move your spotlight around to other areas of your life.

Move your spotlight around.

Healthy Decrees for a Lifetime.

Decree 1. *Abolish toxic thoughts.* Toxic thoughts do not help us. They torment us with our assumption that the worst has happened or will happen.

In this, we incite undue anxiety, unnecessary drama, and waste away the time we could have otherwise enjoyed. Whether the worst has happened or not, it feels as if it has, and we are experiencing the result. When we don't believe in ourselves, we feel less prepared to handle challenging circumstances. The less prepared we feel, the more we fear. Telling ourselves, "I can handle anything that comes at me," can ease our anxiety greatly.

Decree 2. *Turn every negative into a positive.* We have the ability to turn every negative into something productive. Making every hardship into something good is a way of rolling with the punches and turning them into something greater for having had them.

Examples:

Negative: *I can never get ahead.*
Productive: *I am learning patience.*

Negative: *I can't handle this setback.*
Productive: *This will make me wiser for future endeavors.*

Negative: *If I lose, I just can't take it.*
Productive: *I can take whatever comes at me.*

Negative: *If I am found out, I will die.*
Productive: *I am worthy no matter what; I will always be fine.*

Negative: *I can't do it.*
Productive: *I am strong.*

Negative: *I am sick of being abused.*
Productive: *I am going to rescue myself from this situation.*

With productive thinking, we give ourselves directives to harness our personal power and enrich our lives. Thinking productively is in effect, being our own hero. Every time we replace self-defeating internal dialogue with empowering dialogue, we rescue ourselves.

The following techniques can be helpful to incorporate into our daily lives:

Technique 1. Write down your most common negative thoughts. Then tear them up or burn them, making a conscious decision to disallow those thoughts. Then write down productive thoughts, and pin them up somewhere in your house reminding you to think this way.

Technique 2. Inhale the words, slowly and deeply, *I am strong*. Exhale the words, slowly and deeply, *I can handle anything*. For those who can visualize, see yourself in a ball of light. This can strengthen your focus. If visualization isn't the way for you, say the words and really mean them.

Technique 3. Send toxic thoughts into the sun. See them dissolve. Replace them with productive thoughts.

Examples:

I can't do this. Send the thought into sun. See it dissolve. Think, *I can do anything*.

I am afraid of failure. Send the thought into sun. See it dissolve. Think, *Every failure leads to success*.

Productive thinking creates change from the inside out.

It is commonly believed that if we make our outer world change, we will be happier. However, if we practice productive thinking, we can feel better now. When we feel better, we behave in beneficial ways. This changes the reactions of others around us, and hence the quality of our lives. It is far easier to change the way we think than to control what goes on around us.

Changing the way we think is easier
than trying to control what goes on around us.

We can choose our reality.

The choices we make create our reality. The most important choice we can make is choosing how to think.

By accepting that while we can't always control what happens to us, we *can* always control our *response* to what happens to us. From the ashes rises the Phoenix. When we are ready to rise and spread our wings, nothing and no one can stop us.

Points to Remember

1. Our thoughts generate our mood.

2. Our mood influences our actions.

3. Our actions create our reality.

4. Our reality is a product of what we spotlight.

5. Abolish toxic thoughts

6. Replace negative thinking with productive thoughts.

7. Turn every negative into something productive.

8. Control what goes on within you to improve what goes on around you.

9. We control our reality by steering our responses in a productive direction.

4
COMMUNICATE CONSTRUCTIVELY

Constructive communication requires honesty and respect, and can build bridges of understanding between ourselves and others. Our tendency, however, is to hide our *true* thoughts and feelings behind camouflaged walls, opting for modes of expression that are, to say the least, dysfunctional.

All humans have vulnerable areas and issues. Our issues are no less important than anyone else's. We have a right to express ourselves. But *how* we express ourselves can change the outcome of any situation immensely.

When we communicate constructively, we:

   *honor ourselves without dishonoring others

   *purge our upset in a healthy way

   *incite productive evolution in our relationships

   *make discoveries about ourselves

Dysfunctional Communication

Turbulence between people, especially significant others, is largely due to a lack of communication, or ineffective, and/or damaging communication.

Lack of Communication.

There are several reasons we withhold communication.

1. *Fear of confrontation*. We sometimes prefer to sit with a bitter attitude than speak up. The imagined fallout seems more unsavory than keeping our upset a secret. The fallout we fear might be rejection, retaliation, or too much drama.

2. *Avoidance of painful emotions*. Sometimes we survive by *not* stirring the emotional pot.

3. *Upholding the image of perfection*. We might feel we must uphold the image of being perfect in order to be loved, or we like to pretend that we *are* perfect to avoid dealing with deeper issues. Or, we don't want to expose our imperfections or vulnerabilities because we do not trust another with that information.

4. *We want to punish others with the silent treatment*. By building a wall, we are in effect saying, "You can't have my attention unless you behave as I wish."

No matter what the reason, masking our upset results in misunderstanding, continuation of what is triggering the upset, and a mounting anguish that often leads to an unexpected emotional explosion or implosion (hurting self), exacerbating an already tense situation.

Ineffective and/or Damaging Communication.

Communicate don't assassinate. When our primary communication is riddled with criticism, or is combative and accusatory, hotheaded and excessively defensive, or blaming, we are not really communicating, but rather attempting to control or hurt our target.

Criticism

We criticize for several reasons:

1. *To boost our own ego*. Mean spirited criticism is often a defense for a fragile ego, needing to deflate another to inflate ourselves. This is sometimes accompanied by excessive bragging. Bragging is just a way of trying to get others to see how great we are because we want them to like us.

2. *To manipulate*. When we want something from someone and we are not getting it, we might shame them into behaving in a way that serves us.

3. *To be helpful.* When we think we know what is best for another, we may let them know what we think they are doing wrong. While this might come from a good-hearted place, opinions given when not asked for can be interpreted as criticism. The insinuation is that we are more qualified to judge what is right for them than they are.

Criticism is not the same as open-minded sharing what we perceive. When others ask for our honest opinion because they want to better themselves or something in their lives, the honest answer, even if negative, is not usually criticism. Nor is expressing concern for ourselves or a loved one to his or her face. These expressions are a respectful sharing of our point of view because we are worried or we were asked.

Examples of criticism versus sharing:

Criticism: "You didn't clean the dishes well. You really need to do a better job."
Sharing: Kindly saying, "Oh, I see still see gook on that plate."

Criticism: "Your room is still a mess. You are so lazy."
Sharing: "I see your room is still in disarray. I am concerned because company will be here soon."

Criticism: "You really could lose a couple of pounds."
Sharing: "I am concerned about your weight. I am afraid it is making you unhealthy."

Criticism: "You are selfish. You never consider my needs."
Sharing: "I need more from this relationship than I am getting."

Combative and accusatory communication

Some of us have combative or oppositional personalities and don't even realize it. We might get feedback from others that we are attacking them or purposefully causing friction by being confrontational. Our responses to how others reply to what we have said, often have a repelling quality, such as, "That's ridiculous." "You don't know what you are talking about." "You would say that." We are accusing them of, in a sense, behaving badly, when most often, it is we who are behaving badly, or not communicating effectively.

Or we might be combative just because we are disgruntled within ourselves, or life in general. This is often exhibited when we make a comment to someone and no matter what the response, we say something snarky. For example, our mate might say, "I love sunny days," We might respond with, "Sunny days suck. I hate sunny days." It doesn't occur to us to say, "Yes, I know sunny days make you happy." Or our child might say, "I am excited to go to the dance." And we might respond, "Why, so you can get drunk?" It doesn't occur to us to say, "I am excited for you too!"

These combative and accusatory responses create great disturbances in those with whom we relate. Unfortunately, we tend to feel a kind of superiority by doing it, which we seem to need, even if others grow to distain us. We can then accuse them even more of being the one that is wrong, bad, or inferior.

Hotheaded and excessively defensive communication

Hotheaded outbursts and a generally defensive nature are usually an expression of low self-esteem. This anger is commonly steeped in a troubled past, but emerges in the present with attached meanings that have little or nothing to do with our current circumstance.

Barking at others because we are insecure, is a ploy to intimidate them into a passive role. We then feel like the top dog in power, and therefore emotionally safe.

We are defensive even if there is no need to be, and assume those around us are guilty of something even when they are not. For example, if someone pauses before answering a question, we might yell accusingly that he or she is conjuring a lie, when in truth, the pause was about determining the true answer. If our mate is looking out the window at the stars, it might be concluded that a daydream of an old love is being had. If a family member does not want to go into a business deal with us, we might accuse him or her of not trusting us, when it could be that

that deal is just not his or her cup of tea.

Needless to say, this does not bode well for any of our relationships, ultimately sabotaging what we really want, which is to feel safe and loved. Who wants to be around someone who bites! Blowing caustic air instead of productively communicating does nothing but pollute the social environment and drive our relationships further apart.

Blaming

Blaming others is not always hotheaded. Sometimes it is just the way we think. We blame others when they are not behaving how we wish and to deflect responsibility from our part in the matter. Behind the caustic mood is always deeper unrest that we ourselves are not owning. It is easier to take our unresolved issues out on others than to actually resolve them.

For example, if raised in a home where putting on a happy image to the public mattered more than how we really felt, we might feel a need to hide our truths from everyone, and suffer in silence. We then expect everyone around us to do the same. Suck it up and shut up. If they do not, we blame them. The real issue is that we ourselves were scarred by that standard growing up and have not released the need to live up to it. We then force our learned behavior on others even when it hurts them.

In this example, even though we may wish our parents would have valued our feelings more than our public image, our learned behavior has become a standard we innately set for others, most commonly our children. Our parents blamed us for not performing a certain way because they were insecure, and so we blame our children for not performing a certain way because we are insecure.

If we don't look at our unhealthy learned behavior, and instead blame others for our feelings, we continue the cycle. The good news is, these behaviors can be unlearned with relative ease by constructively communicating what is true and real for us, and in turn, allowing others to communicate what is true and real for them.

The Best Way to Communicate

When communicating, treat others the way you wish to be treated. Do not expect others to change their behavior to make you feel better. Change might come, but communicating effectively is primarily for you. Communicate to honor yourself, purge toxic emotions, and prevent misunderstandings that might lead to unsavory consequences. Ultimately, it might be you who has to make some changes in your life to feel better.

Once you share, then the ball is in the other person's court. What they do with it is up to them.

Rules for constructive communication:

1. Calm down (do your breathing).

2. Know your worth (speak up out of self-respect).

3. Think productively (I want to improve relations, not make them worse.)

4. Describe the upsetting event. *When you laughed at me. . . When you canceled our date. . . When you tell me you will do something but don't . . .*

5. Share what emotion that situation evoked without blaming. *When you . . . I felt sad, unloved, angry, scared, insecure, stupid, shocked, etc.*

6. If you can, share why you feel the way you feel regarding that occurrence. It is not always necessary to say why we feel the way we do, but if we can, it lends more understanding, not only to whom we are speaking, but also to ourselves. This is because, to express the truth, we have to dig deep to figure out what we are trying to say. Examples: *When you . . . I felt . . . because I am sensitive about that*, or *because I need more in a relationship*, or *because I deserve better treatment*, or *because I work hard to make things nice*, or *because I am afraid you will leave me.*

Examples of constructive communication:

Description of event: *When you told me I could lose a few pounds . . .* Your feeling: *I felt upset . . .* Why: *because I am sensitive about my weight.*

Description of event: *When you told me you were going to a movie, but went to a party . . .* Your feeling: *I felt devastated . . .* why: *because I always thought I could trust you.*

Examples of putting it all together:

When you flirted with that woman, I felt disrespected, because I am your sexual partner and it seems you want her too.

When you avoid spending time with me, I feel upset, because without that emotional intimacy, I feel our relationship slipping away.

If the person gets defensive say something like, *I don't expect you to do anything differently. I am just sharing how I feel.*

Resist the impulse to strike back, or get into a recycled argument, or to push the other to change. When people change to please others and not to improve themselves, it is always short lived. Making another aware gives that person an opportunity to perhaps work on their issues. But they may pass on that.

If you must react, repeat what you said a time or two, then shift the subject by saying something like, *Well, I shared what was going on with me, now I am going to . . .* Could be take a walk, get to work, go to bed. You are just letting the other person know you aren't willing to argue, you just wanted to honestly communicate your upset.

After that, despite the response, take a deep breath, let it go, you did your part. Now go do something that makes you feel better.

If there is an interest to learn more about what you are sharing, further productive dialogue can ensue.

Respectful, honest communication is healing for all, even if others do not respond the way we wish. It is not about blame, or who is wrong or right. We feel the way we feel and that is that. We are simply communicating our reality to another. In this, we often make important self-discoveries.

Granted, when deeply hurt or angered, it is often difficult to communicate constructively even if we know how. However, if we can take a deep breath, step forward and speak our truth—we will experience a kind of proclamation in who we are, a spreading of wings, so to speak.

Sharing who we are is a crucial step in having healthy relationships with others, and more importantly, with ourselves.

A Word of Caution:

If in a relationship with a seemingly unstable or dangerous person, effort to communicate will do little to no good. Consider finding a *safe* way to either end the relationship (might mean going to a shelter) or if possible get them help. Do all this in a calm manner. Do not taunt or argue with this person. They likely are not capable of a healthy response.

No matter how much we might want to save another, they must want to save themselves and make constructive changes in their life, rather than trying to turn us into a robot who will satisfy their every need, including someone to blame.

No matter what we say, we will almost assuredly be misinterpreted by the mentally disturbed person.

Points to Remember

1. Communicate to honor yourself, purge toxic feelings, and prevent misunderstanding.

2. Don't expect others to change their behavior to make you feel better, however, be prepared to productively change yours.

3. Communicate, don't assassinate.

4. Communicate respectfully; treat others as you wish to be treated.

5. To communicate productively: describe the upsetting occurrence, the emotion evoked, and if applicable, the reason for your reaction.

6. Communicate, then take healthy responsibility to feel better.

5

LISTEN

The other side of productive communication is listening. Human beings have a great need to be heard. When we are heard, we feel validated. When we are validated, we feel alive.

When we are not acknowledged as a living, breathing human being who matters as a unique individual, something inside us starts to die. We feel lonely. Those who are alone too long begin to feel as if they don't exist.

When we speak, but are not heard, or when others speak and we don't hear them, the cry to be acknowledged falls on deaf ears. We frequently get so fired up to express our point of view that we bombard those trying to express theirs.

When two people get locked into wanting to be heard and no one is listening, a battle brews and can get so enflamed, the only result is a riff in the relationship.

Every burst of insistence to be heard without listening to others comes from a desperate need to be validated, despite the topic. In fact, arguments are less about the topic than just needing to be warmly recognized. We all express ourselves in various ways, but the core of what we are trying to say *always* has meaning.

When we listen to each other, that meaning can be unearthed, revealing who we are behind the masks we feel we must wear to survive in the world. When we respectfully listen to others and validate that we have heard them, remarkable things can happen.

When we practice good listening habits, we:

* create precious bonds with others

* are more deeply appreciated

* are more likely to be heard

* aid others in their own self-discovery

* enable others to find their own solutions

* begin to see and appreciate other people's truths

* better understand our loved ones

* fruitfully develop relationships

What *Not* to Do

When we *interrupt* the speaker with a defensive response, criticism, or unasked for solutions, the chance for deeper bonding is quashed along with the opportunity for productive communication. When we show disrespect to another's sharing, there is always friction and turmoil, just as there is with us when our expression has been trashed.

Telling people they shouldn't feel a certain way is also a bond breaker. All our feelings have rhyme and reason, even we don't understand them. We feel what we feel, and we can't feel better until we begin expressing from where we are at.

What to Do

Listen. Let others know that their point of view is understood. Do this by summarizing what they are saying *without* interjecting thoughts and feelings of your own.

Example: Your child says, "I hate everyone at school; they are mean. I don't want to go to school anymore."

Summary Response: "You don't want to go to school anymore because people are mean."

Child: "Yes. Everybody hates me."

Summary Response: "You think nobody likes you."

Child: "Well, one person likes me."

Summary Response: "So not everybody hates you."

Child: "Some people like me; it's just the bullies who hate me and make me feel bad."

Summary Response: "So only the bullies hate you."

Child: "Yes."

Everything the child says then, just summarize until he or she is finished. After all is said and done, you can add your thoughts. For example, "It sounds hard for you. I am sorry you have to go through that. I love you."

Just being empathetically heard and getting an affirmation of love is immensely helpful whether or not solutions are generated. However, once others feel heard, they tend to relax and are more likely to consider solutions, yours, or maybe even their own. *What can we do about this? i*s a great opener for both parties to generate ideas.

Even if the sharing is a complaint about us, listening can turn everything to our favor. Either we can better understand how our behavior is affecting that person, or we might be able to clear up a misunderstanding.

Learning to listen, whether we agree or not with the speaker, will not only improve that relationship, but challenge us to open our minds to understand where others are coming from. In this, our relationships grow more harmonious.

Example: Your child is yelling at you.

Child: "I don't ever want to see you again!"

Summary Response: "You sound like you are sick of me."

Child: "I *am* sick of you. You never let me go anywhere."

Summary Response: "You think I keep you home too much."

Child: "You do, you don't trust me!"

Summary Response: "You think I keep you home because I don't trust you."

Child: "You *don't* trust me."

Whenever the person finally falls silent with nothing more to say, seemingly finished expressing, you can respond respectfully.

For example, "I do trust you; it's everyone else I don't trust. I love you so much and it is my job to keep you safe. But I hear you. You really want to get out more."

If the person starts emoting again, then again respond in summary.

At the end of the conversation, you both can share suggestions that suit you both, then strike a compromise. In the example above, it might be that you together come up with a list of safe places your child can go.

Constructive listening not only involves validating what a person is saying, but can also be a reflection of what he or she is doing.

Example: Your mate is slumped on the couch looking sad.

Summary Response: "You look upset."

Mate: "Yes, I had a bad day."

Summary Response: "So bad things happened to you today."

Mate: "Yes, my boss . . ."

Whatever the response, keep the summary going without inserting your thoughts or feelings.

The goal is not to save the other, but by being heard we boost the opportunity for him or her to save themselves.

The conversation may or may not go far. Don't push it. Your real message is: *I am here, and I will listen.* You are inviting that person to honestly share without being judged, attacked, or demeaned. Once your significant other knows that he or she can open up and communicate with you, and actually be heard—then constructive communication in the future is imminent.

When we listen and reflect back to the speaker what they are saying, often the speaker will find their own solution in hearing themselves talk. When we draw them out and make them feel safe to share, they better understand themselves. When we give validity to their thoughts and feelings, their self-esteem is boosted and they have a clearer point of view.

If we handled our communications and our listening this effectively, all our relationships would improve.

A Word of Caution.

If those we listen to are incessantly abusive, consider getting distance in the relationship in the safest, healthiest way possible. We need *never* tolerate abuse, and we owe it to ourselves to disconnect from chronic abusers. If we allow this behavior, we are not only sacrificing our lives to the abuser, but encouraging him or her to continue the maltreatment. Abusers are conflicted internally and never get better when they are rewarded for ill behavior. In short, we aren't doing them any favors.

Points to Remember

1. Listening to others can forge powerful bonds, especially with our loved ones.

2. When people feel heard, they calm down and feel closer to the listener.

3. Letting others know they are heard without judgment is more helpful than offering solutions, although that can have its place after all is expressed.

4. We can be better heard, if we first listen, even if what we hear upsets us.

5. People need to be heard and acknowledged in a comforting manner, such as, "That must be hard for you. Yes, I understand." Or, "Now I have an idea what you are going through."

6. Respect the views of others even when we don't agree.

7. Let others know we hear them by empathetically summarizing what they seem to be expressing. When that is done, we can then

express our views in a non-blaming way.

8. Never tolerate abuse. Find a safe way to distance yourself from a chronic abuser.

6
TAKE CHARGE OF YOUR LIFE

It is no one's job to make us happy, and it is not our job to make others happy. We are responsible for our own happiness, and others are responsible for theirs. While helping each other can be beneficial, appreciated, and sometimes necessary, it is up to us to steer our own ship and not blame others for how we feel because *we* put them at the helm.

When we take charge of our lives, we:

   *have the courage to champion ourselves

   *feel more joyful about living

   *do not succumb to the wishes of others if it is hurting us

   *stop hiding behind others

   *stop avoiding healthy confrontation

   *welcome personal growth

Depending on Others to Feel Better

In the course of our lives, there are times when we might lament about our circumstance, feeling helpless to change it, and thus trapped, left to battle depression, anxiety, grumpiness, and prolonged stress.

The circumstance might involve a myriad of unsavory elements: monetary troubles, unsatisfactory relationships, physical image, poor health, legal trouble, boredom, or even a withering of our spirit from lack of being nurtured. We often hope for something good to happen to us, or for someone to rescue us from our woe.

When our happiness depends on pleasant occurrences or others to perform in certain ways, we develop a host of reasons why we can't feel better, unless those things happen. In this, we remain at an impasse that keeps us in our self-made prison. Without realizing it, we often develop an unproductive persona that suppresses our true self.

The Zombie

When we go through the motions but feel dead inside, we are the Zombie. We are doing what we feel we are supposed to do, suppressing our true needs. Getting the job done is all that matters. Everything looks good on paper, but inside, we are suffering.

The folly in this is that we typically grow increasingly depressed. Sometimes, the depression drags us into a deep dark hole and we can't get out. Allowing logic to rule our lives, our emotions are repressed, and if not addressed, will develop into some rather ugly feelings that will eventually surface in an unsavory manner.

The Pack Mule

When we succumb to the wishes of others to the detriment of our self, we are the Pack Mule. We do our best to make everyone else happy. We might appear all right, but in truth, are deeply sad within ourselves.

The folly in this is that we have a growing resentment that no one seems to care about what makes *us* happy. Eventually, something deep inside us cries out, and we snap, acting in extremes that express our unbearable upset.

The Martyr.

When we step up to the plate, and happily try to do everything for everyone, and practically nothing for ourselves, we are the Martyr. We tend to over empathize, taking on the problems or discomfort of others as our own. Our sense of worth is predicated on helping others, and we feel they cannot be okay without our help, nurturing, and sacrifice.

The folly in this is that our energy output not only leaves us depleted, but we are so focused on the lives of others, our own personal growth is stunted. So is theirs. If those we continually help did more for themselves, they would develop the self-confidence needed to make their own way in the world. And if we did more for ourselves, we would experience new and great vistas of self-discovery.

The Shadow

When we make another the center of our lives, we become their shadow. We live to please that person, going along with his or her every opinion and decision, because we are too afraid to step out into the world to pave our own way, and take responsibility for our mistakes. We take comfort in the shelter of that person's persona and worship their existence above all others.

The folly in this is that we never discover who we are, and thus do not grow into what we could be. We live in fear of losing the relationship, needing someone to spearhead our life. And our other relationships, having been deemed less important, are of questionable quality.

The Victim

When we have a chronic attitude that others have it better than us, and therefore should offer us aid and sympathy, we are the Victim. We live to be saved because it is a proven way to get confirmation of our worth. Being saved is equated with being loved.

> *The chronic victim equates*
> *being saved with being loved.*

The saving might be in the form of time, energy, money, or love. If we don't get help or those who have been helping, stop, we condemn them. They could help us, but they won't. Our suffering is *their* fault. We are ever the victim, waiting to be rescued over and over again. We do not need to change *our* behavior, but we believe those around us, should.

The folly in this is that no one can save us. We can be helped, but not saved. Receiving help from time to time is healthy when we use it to better our lives. If we don't, then we are inciting help from others as a band-aid to get us through the day, rather than actually taking action to solve our problems. Dependent on others to soothe our ills, we never learn to rely on ourselves. We not only deplete those helping us, but we cheat ourselves out of growing strong and experiencing the freedom of self-reliance.

The Director

When we attempt to take charge of other people's lives to do the work we could or should be doing ourselves, we are the Director. Example: We want our son to be a professional (so we can feel like a success), or our grown daughter to call and visit often (to assuage our loneliness), or our mate to shower us with attention (to affirm our worth). We might even allocate all the work to be done to those around us, leaving us to do nothing but direct.

The folly in this is that we can't really win. If those whom we direct are strong-willed and don't comply, we feel anxious. If they do comply, eventually resentment brews because they are suppressing what is right for them, to act in ways that are right for us. And if they stop behaving the way we want, we accuse them of not caring about us. How dare they go off the rails and fall down on the job of making us happy! Until we face what we fear and develop our own lives instead of directing others, we will ever feel uneasy and sad about our stressed relationships.

The Illusionist

The Illusionist is like the Director, with one major difference. While the Director is obvious in spouting expectations, the Illusionist is masterfully subtle. We are the Illusionist when our subjects don't realize they are being manipulated into satisfying our needs. Our tools are inciting guilt, shame, or a feeling of ineptitude. Guilt: "I feel sick if I don't eat home cooked meals three times a day." Shame: "All my friends have a cleaner house than ours." Ineptitude: "You don't make enough money for us to go have fun."

The folly in this is that because we rely on others to satisfy our needs, we are always on edge because we remain dependent on them to keep it up. Keep the house spotless *for me*. Keep bringing in money *for me*. Keep winning awards *for me*. *Shower me* with compliments. *Cook me* wonderful meals. *Make me* look good to the public. Put on a good image *for me*. Eventually our subjects will need to, and quite rightly, rebel and do what they must for *themselves*.

Rescuing Ourselves

While we generally prefer others give us what we want, rather than earn it for ourselves, or blame others for our woe, rather than doing something about it, there is no forward movement in our personal development.

When we release others from the mandate that they must save us or serve us, and begin doing those things for ourselves, we jumpstart our personal growth.

*Release others from the mandate
that they must save us or serve us.*

In taking responsibility for our own fulfillment, not only will our relationships improve, but we will begin to discover a deeper happiness than we could ever imagine, for our content is not in the hands of another, but in our own. We all have the ability to rise, even from parched or violent settings. But we must take charge of our reality. That is the only way we can change it.

How to Take Charge of Your Life

Taking charge of our lives begins with a simple question, *What healthy step can I take right now to feel better?*

The answer might be to take a stroll, jog, swim, or shower, express pent up feelings, or maybe *not* to react to something. Then do that. After that, ask the question again, *What healthy step can I take right now to feel better*? Continue the process. Small steps lead to bigger actions, and will eventually walk us right out of our quagmire into a more fulfilling life direction.

For example, you might feel a walk would do you good. After taking the walk, your metabolism is boosted. You are now in a better mood and decide to finish that woodworking project you started. Enjoying your creativity, your spirits are further brightened. This then puts you into the mood to sign up for that furniture-making class you have been wanting to take. That class might inspire a new career. On and on it goes.

When we allow the question, *What healthy thing can I do right now to feel better,* to guide our lives, we begin to pave a one of a kind path that is right for us, and maybe only us. Moment by moment, day by day, one step at a time, we can be resolved to always move in the direction that feels healthiest. In this, we are taking responsibility for our own unhappiness.

If we don't take healthy steps, we resort to quick fixes to get us through the day, for example, drugs and alcohol, overeating, or overspending. These band-aids are about covering up pain, rather than healing it, and are ultimately destructive.

Healthy choices do not harm others.

Our quest to feel better is never at the expense of our well-being or others, such as going into unnecessary debt, barking at our loved ones, ignoring our children, or having an affair.

This doesn't mean those around us may not object to the productive changes we are making. We might receive complaints that we are doing less for them, and be called selfish. This is just an attempt to get things back the way they were.

Example: The night class you are taking is met with protest from your spouse because you aren't around to tend the kids, and the kids claim you don't care about them as much. These sort of objections are often rooted in fear that the positive steps you are taking for yourself will lead you away from them. However, the uprising can be calmly met with something like, "I need to do this for me."

Eventually, they will see that you are happier, and thus more loving and pleasant to be around. Realizing you are still there for them, they'll calm down and feel more secure.

Even if others are displeased with our healthy behavior, the fact that we can't be manipulated as once we were, will generate respect, mostly because we are respecting ourselves. We also become an excellent role model, showing others that they too have a right to take care of themselves. Our constructive behaviors will continue to ripple forth and do good for the world.

The power of attraction begins within us.

When we take steps to give *ourselves* what we need to grow and flourish, we not only change what happens to us, but we also attract more psychologically healthy people into our lives.

There is a common misnomer in our social world that we're nobody until somebody loves us. But actually, it is the opposite. When we love ourselves, many quite easily admire and love us too. Our experiences are more pleasant and opportunities rise.

Harness personal power.

We ourselves, have the answers to our problems, all of them, if we but calm down, and turn inward to find them. No matter what has happened to us or how others treat us, we cannot be stopped from growing into our full potential, unless we stop ourselves. We are each unique. No two of us are the same. The only life path right for us is the one we pave.

Points to Remember

1. Take responsibility for your unhappiness by taking healthy steps to feel better.

2. Fulfill your own needs, and support others fulfilling theirs.

3. Help others help themselves, and receive help to help yourself.

4. Use personal power to spearhead your life; be your own hero.

7
BE YOUR OWN PERSON

Hand in hand with taking charge of our lives is becoming our own person. As no two people are alike, we each perceive reality through a unique lens. This means that reality for each of the billions of people on earth is not *exactly* the same. Given this, neither is our life path. Not exactly.

However, the world out there can be quite daunting, and out of a need to survive, we often adopt other people's ways to be accepted by them. If we belong to a group, even a small one, we feel more secure. That is human nature.

Given this, we are prone to emulating others. The more we do it, the less devotion we have in being ourselves. The further away we get from who we uniquely are, the worse we feel. When we disregard our own thoughts and feelings, we feel lost inside, like being in a room with fogged up windows, or in a time out in our own life. We have put ourselves at the mercy of others, and our true potential is locked away in a vault that no other can see.

To be our own person is to have the guts to truly live as a free thinking individual. Are we living our hopes and dreams, or suppressing them to render approval from others? Are we discovering and expressing our uniqueness, or are we emulating those who embody who we *think* we should be?

We all have different ways of doing things, ways that might be right for us but nobody else. Until we get brave and do what feels healthiest for us at any given moment, we are quite literally forfeiting our own becoming. We are the caterpillar in the cocoon that never sees the light of day.

In allowing ourselves to discover, through trial and error, what works for us and what does not, we begin to celebrate our uniqueness. In short, we begin to like ourselves—deeply.

When we are our own person, we:

*nourish our individuality

*discover who we truly are

*foster personal growth

*can make important stands

*meet our challenges with greater success

*feel clear and bright inside

*forge a satisfying life path

Our intellect can work against us.

While the animal kingdom imitates to learn, and reacts to the social rules of that genus, the human intellect, while rocketing us to the top of the food chain, also feeds our head with psychological misnomers that keep us bumping into walls, for example, the older we get, the more worthless we become.

This high tech world we live in further complicates our mind processes. We are exposed to thousands of differing views that can enrich us, yet also make the world seem chaotic. Constantly showered with stimuli, other people's beliefs, troubles, manipulations, and needs, our attention can be easily diverted. Before we know it, we are lured off our unique life path onto somebody else's, and living out another's idea of what *our* reality should be.

Living someone else's reality, or for a group's ideology occurs for several reasons:

1. We need to ease our suffering; we need it fast, and we need it now.

2. We are desperate for a life direction.

3. We need approval from others to approve of ourselves.

4. We put others above us, demeaning ourselves.

5. We fear betting on ourselves.

Be aware if adopted ideologies are not right for you.

When we tap into other peoples' ideologies, thinking them our own or making them our own, it may or may not be healthy for us. When we need approval from others, we are having difficulty approving of ourselves. We feel insecure and have a need to belong, to be accepted, and in some regard, loved, and may even sacrifice our individuality to get it. Hence, we adopt the beliefs of those whom we want to sanction our worth.

The folly in this is that we abandon our true self to hitch our wagon to another who seems to be paving "a" way. We might feel safer hiding in the fold of another or others, but that *deep down* lost feeling remains.

Yet, sometimes in the wake of following others, we can still find ways to be ourselves, if those others closely resonate to who we are. If that ideology works for us, and our life is flourishing, then it is serving a productive purpose. Feeling that we are in our element, and have found our tribe, our attitude is positive and bright.

If the ideology is hurting us in some way, (if something doesn't sit well with us) perhaps even stalling us from growing, then shifting focus to our deep, true inner self, can serve as a homing beacon to set ourselves right again.

Nourish yourself first.

When we metaphorically starve ourselves to care for others, we are deeming them more important than us. When we always put others first, we eventually run out of steam, and then we can't help anyone. Sometimes, without realizing it, we are psycholigically sabateuging ourselves, encouraging others to become their own person so that we don't have to become ours. We can wait. Yet, behind that wait, there often lurks a fear of discovering our true self. What if it isn't good?

The folly in this is that we are always left with the short end of the stick, unable to foster our personal growth from lack of nourishment. We feel uncomfortable focusing on our needs. Hence, our true self will ever be a mystery.

Step out of the cave.

Living in the shadow of others is often easier than stepping out of the cave to examine in the pure light of day who we really are. If we are the costar in someone else's life or ideology, we can't make mistakes, because if anything goes wrong it is always the fault of the person or group we are following.

The folly in this is that somewhere inside us is a lack of belief in our personal power. We don't think we can believe in it, so we abdicate to others and sacrifice having our own adventure to instead tag along on theirs. So, we always feel a little lost, or not altogether like ourselves.

If in stepping out of our cave and exposing our true self, we falter, that is okay. It will only be a matter of time before we gain our footing and begin to be inspired by our new adventure.

It's okay to err in the quest
to discover our true self.

Be the star in your own show.

When we become the sidekick in someone else's life, we have in effect, become the costar of our own show. Becoming the star requires authenticity, and courage. What do we really think about this or that? When we begin to speak and act on our own behalf, we begin to define our personality, such as, we love horses, or have a penchant for cooking, or for building things, or for justice, or for politics, or the arts. We become a radiant jewel, captivating and interesting in our own right. We are our own person! We are then taking back our life and becoming the star of our own show.

This may or may not be in harmony with our partners, significant others, or community groups. Either way, that lost, scattered, deprived, sad or grumpy feeling will disappear. If this takes us away from someone in our life, it will also give us new and better suited alliances in the long run.

It's not about being normal.

Forget trying to be normal. Normal can be the death of what is unique and best in us. The term normal only means our behavior is within the norm, within the scope of what most people are doing. It doesn't mean that the behavior of the masses is healthy. Sometimes to spread our wings, we just have to be ourselves, even if we stick out like a sore thumb.

If no one was ever true to themselves, we wouldn't have traveled to outer space, or have airplanes, inventions, art, literature, or theater. Women would have no vote, and minorities no rights. Democratic countries would not even be free if the originators didn't follow their truth and break off from the norm.

Just like a seed that grows into a tree, we too are meant to unfold into our own greatness.

Champion your true self.

When we are our own person, on our own unique path, we feel empowered and contented. An enthusiastic charge fills our body, mind, and heart. All the mysteries of life that we seek answers to are experienced beyond understanding, and even explaining. We just feel good from deep down inside, like a drug induced, yet drug free brightness from within. This is what it is like to be centered. No matter what commotion swirls around us, all is well.

Remaining centered in ourselves on a quest of personal growth, keeps us moving toward self-actualization, which is the process of growing into our full fruition.

We usually must fight for this. Just as our significant others might at first protest when we take charge of our lives, so might they when we develop into our true selves, expressing our genuine thoughts and feelings. They might react negatively to get us to be who they want us to be, who they are used to us being.

When this happens, they are just afraid for us or themselves because the status quo is changing. How will these changes affect everything?

When we change, we also incite change upon those around us. They may have to do more or different things, and they'd rather not. If we remain strong, and keep nourishing our uniqueness in healthy ways, no matter what caterwauling, threats, demands, peacock strutting, or pleading is going on around us, we will blossom.

If we act on what makes us feel joyful, clear, and enthusiastic, then we can stay on our path, and still be loving toward others.

To begin, we must be aware of our deep down yearnings.

Address deep down yearnings.

Along with asking the question, *what healthy thing can I do right now to feel better*, we must listen to our deep down yearnings, which at their root, are akin to crying out for food or water. *I am here. I am me. I matter!*

"I" is unique. When we nourish this uniqueness we begin to come into our own. If, for example, we yearn to have genuine connections with others, then create that circumstance by perhaps volunteering, or taking in a foster child. If we are dying for creative expression, then sing, dance, paint, write, decorate, or create something.

As we begin to satisfy our deep down yearnings in a healthy way, who we are becomes more clear. We start to distinguish what *we* need from what others *tell us* we need. We begin to feel *who we are* and slowly leave behind what others *expect us to be*.

> *Let go of who you think you should be
> and become who you are.*

Only when we each grow into ourselves, like a puzzle piece unique to all others, can we fit together and make a picture that makes sense. As long as we keep adopting or supporting other people's ways or beliefs when they do *not* resonate with our inner being, we will generate unhealthy interactions.

When we are true to ourselves, we help the world.

What is good for us will benefit countless others.

Unless compelled to step into the social or global stage, much good can come from simply focusing on our own backyard, growing into all we can be, and letting the rest of the world's problems go.

Bringing our own life into fruition will positively affect thousands of people in our lifetime. We each are invaluably important even if we don't make the news or history books. It is often the smallest of interactions that have the greatest value.

Here are some examples: saving an abandoned animal; believing in someone; kindly smiling at that overworked store clerk; listening to the life story of an old woman; playing with a child; kicking that bad habit, sharing kind thoughts and feelings about others to their face; using constructive communication; or even waving at a neighbor. These kinds of interactions are at the root of what eventually manifests in the world as great goodness.

The greatest example we can be to anyone is to genuinely be our own person and follow our own path with dedication and dignity. In that, we find comfort, and are in our greatest and most magnificent form.

Points to Remember

1. Think for yourself.

2. Address your deep down yearnings in a healthy manner.

3. Nurture yourself first.

4. Nourish your uniqueness to grow into all you can be.

5. When we are our own person, we better the world.

Handling Emotions

8
USE ANGER WISELY

Getting angry is normal and healthy. What we do with it will determine an improvement or deterioration in our life condition. When angry, we want to lash out, sometimes only in our minds (play out scenes but don't do anything), sometimes passive aggressively (punish the offender, but never say why), sometimes outright (vocally and/or physically emoting raw feelings). And sometimes, we lash ourselves. We can however, make anger work for us to improve our lives.

Make anger work for you, not against you.

Anger is a constructive emotion when used as a motivator to make us do better. For instance, standing up for ourselves, or climbing out of an unhealthy situation.

Anger is constructive when we have just had enough of something, like our house falling apart, or a dead end job, and we get on the bandwagon to make improvements.

We use anger constructively when we protect ourselves or someone else from a bully or a predator.

In all these cases, anger is the indicator that something is wrong, and we are taking responsibility to make it right.

When we use anger wisely, we:

   *make our anger work for us, not against us

   *use it to make productive stands to improve our lives

   *realize our anger may be a symptom of a deeper issue

   *take responsibility to feel better, and not cast blame

   *do not take our upset out on others

   *use it defend others

   *gain self-respect

   *feel our personal power

Destructive anger works against us.

While our reasons for anger vary, all anger (aside from a chemical imbalance) is rooted in pain, caused by feeling insulted, assaulted, or afraid. We might repress anger and let if fester, fearing the consequences of letting it out. This is destructive to our body and general well-being. Or, we might explode in frequent knee jerk reactions to shield our hearts, causing others to shield theirs.

Anger works against us when we:

1. *Spit our rage on innocent others*. Example: We just got rejected for a job and our child wants to play with us. We bark, "Go away, not now!"

2. *Hold others responsible for our anger*. Example: "I hate how you always repeat yourself. You really bug me!"

3. *Anger at those who do not behave as we wish*. Example: "You don't want to have sex, fine. I'll go find somebody else!"

4. *Are mad that others take care of themselves instead of us*. Example: "You don't need to take that night class; you should be home with me. You are just being selfish."

5. *Blame others for our mistakes*. Example: "You should have reminded to pay that bill!"

6. *Martyr ourselves, then complain we are not appreciated.* Example: "I surprise you by spending all day making this gourmet meal and you don't even care!"

7. *Let it fester.* Example: "She's always picking on me. One day I will tell her just what I think of her!"

8. *Are bio chemically off balance.* We might feel chronically angry even if things are going great in our lives. In this case, it can be helpful to see a health care professional to determine if there is something going on in our body, in addition to learning how to channel anger in more productive ways.

The Blame Game

Blaming, quite efficiently, deflects pain from us and hurls it upon others. The less resolved we are with our issues, the more defensive (angry) we become. For example, we might assume people are criticizing us, even if they are not. Or, if sensitive about feeling dumb, we twist almost anything anyone says into an insult that we are stupid. Or, if we are sensitive about being poor, we might assume everyone is looking down their nose at us, even if they are looking up.

Blaming others is also a way of excusing ourselves from taking any responsibility to change what is upsetting us.

Blaming can be disguised in a number of masks:

Sacrificial Blamers

When we deplete ourselves to make others feel better, but pout when we don't get desired results, we are Sacrificial Blamers. Example: *My gift didn't make her happy; she doesn't even care about all the work I put into it.* Or, *he didn't care that I spent all day cleaning his room; he is so unappreciative.*

The folly in this is that instead of making the receivers feel better, they are made to feel guilty, and at fault for not making *us* feel better. Our good deeds have an underlying motive to boost our own spirits. Until we can take actions to make ourselves feel better, this pattern will never end.

Rage Spitters

We are Rage Spitters when we want others to back off. We view them as an opponent we must attack and defeat to keep them under our thumb and away from our hearts. This way they can't hurt us. We get them before there is any possibility that they can get us. There is no room for communication or understanding. Oh, we want them around, but not too close. If we have chased them too far away, we reel them back in with a bit of kindness, but always ready with a wad of toxic rage to spit if they trespass the boundary we have set around ourselves.

The folly in this 'throwing up' on others is that the loving attention we need from them to heal our damaged heart is sabotaged because eventually our targets just don't want to be around us anymore. Our behavior reflects personal problems we do not want to admit are there. Feeling the pain is too much. It is easier to make others feel the pain that is ours.

When we allow anger to control our lives as a sword and shield to cloak our heart, we find ourselves in constant battle with nearly everyone, and nearly always. Significant others, colleagues, bosses, even strangers. We are always at war, feeling we must be if we are to survive. Until we can find another way to cope with our anger, we will have difficulty sustaining healthy relationships.

Control Freaks

We Control Freaks only feel the world is right if we can control our environment and the people in our lives. When we are in control, we feel safe. Rage Spitters might be Control Freaks, but not all Control Freaks spit rage. Some of us are emotionally controlling, using more quiet and well planned means to meet our ends.

When things don't go our way or people don't behave the way we need, we get anxious and use subtle intimidation to make those who have gone off script get back on it to do our bidding. Example: One spouse says to the other almost playfully, "If you don't lose weight, I might have to find a sexier mate." The message is, *Lose weight, or else*. Or saying to a child, "If you don't clean your room, I am going to spank you." The message is, *Do as I tell you or I will hurt you*. (This message can get manifest in adulthood as physical abuse).

Control Freaks also feel ire toward anyone connected to whatever is going wrong. For example, if our washing machine breaks down, it is the fault of the last person who used it, even if it was used correctly.

The folly in this is that our relationships slowly deteriorate. In addition, when we control others, we almost always stunt their personal growth because we are so busy getting them to be what we want them to be, that we don't allow them to grow into who they are. We also stunt our own personal growth by never facing *why* it is so important to be in control of everything and everyone around us.

When others see us coming, they usually learn to get out of the line of fire just to have a little hidden corner where they can be themselves. In time, they might secretly find other ways to get their needs met. Until we can respect the needs of others and support their way of doing things, our relating remains unproductive, even if we manage to manipulate them to achieve our expectations.

Our old upsets can surface in the present.

We are all psychologically wounded to some degree because life is life. However, some of us have healed our wounds mostly or all together, and others of us hide our wound as if it isn't there. But it is there, always raw, and when poked even unintentionally, we get easily grumpy, bitey, and short-tempered about what has nothing to do with what is actually occurring in our present life. In other words, we take our old emotional injuries out on those around us.

However, whether our anger is from the past or in the present, it can be transformed into something productive.

Transforming Destructive Anger.

If chronic anger is an issue with us, it is essential that we take healthy steps to deal with it. Otherwise, we will blame innocent others, and eventually chase them out of our lives.

Once we constructively deal with it, much anger will subside, and if any is left, it is because there is some healthy action we need to take to champion our honor. This is not about manipulating others to change their behavior. It is about making an honorable stand for ourselves to help us shake off the insult or assault.

Dealing with destructive anger can be done by taking the following steps:

1. Calm down *before* expressing upset.

When you feel you are about to lose it, stop, step back, close your eyes. Breathe deeply, slowly, and steadily. See a beautiful blue, green, or purple (calming colors) light fill your body. Visualize yourself in a favorite soothing place all alone and safe. Nothing can hurt you. You have everything you need. You feel your worth. Say to yourself, "I want to make things better not worse."

2. Open your mind.

Realize that just because you *think* something doesn't make it true. If for example, you conclude someone doesn't care about you, rephrase your thinking. *I could be wrong. Maybe the truth is not what I'm thinking.* Examples: *I don't know for* sure if my son did that purposely, maybe he didn't. Or, *I don't know for sure if she cheated on me, maybe she didn't.*

As previously stated, we all create interpretations based on our *perceptions* and then react accordingly. Yet, no matter how firmly we believe our interpretations are correct, they are based on guesswork. And even if we are right, when we understand the motive of those that seem to hurt us, we often have a different picture of the event altogether!

3. Put things in perspective.

Example: You are working on your car, and you ask your mate to bring your toolbox. Your mate sets the box on top of the trunk and scuffs the wax finish. You snap and accuse her of scuffing your car as if done on purpose. Consider the person's intent. Was it to upset you, or hand you the box you asked for? If her intent was to do something nice for you and you yell at her, what do you suppose that will do to the relationship? *Intent matters.* If someone angers you but had good intention, putting the intention first can quit literally save the relationship.

4. Replace self-defeating thoughts with productive thoughts.

For instance, replace lines like: *he took advantage of me; she abused me; people are destroying the earth; he doesn't care about me; she treats me like garbage; they are trying to destroy me, control me, make me be their puppet; they are slandering me, making fun of me, treating me like I am bad or don't matter,* with productive lines such as these:

I like myself. Think of your unique strengths.

I love myself. Feel compassion for all you have endured.

I am strong. Say, "I can handle anything that comes at me."

My worth is invaluable. Feel yourself walking proud and strong along a beach, climbing a mountain, even soaring in the sky or universe. Feel your worth far far away from other people's opinions.

5. Consider sharing what you are experiencing with another who is not involved in the event.

Venting with another person can be extremely healthy, as long we don't get stuck there, looping for hours, days, months, or years. Initial venting helps us clarify what we are feeling and thinking, before making a connection with whom we are upset. If we choose an open minded, non-judgmental person, we can often determine if we are over reacting, casting unfair blame, or if it is time to take a productive stand. If the later is determined, effective communication can be practiced. If we have no one in our life like that, a mental health professional is an option.

6. Constructively air grievances.

If or when the time comes to express our anger with whom we have issue, constructively and respectfully air your upset. Express what you are experiencing in an open-minded way, remembering that just because we think something doesn't make it true. Apply constructive communication skills, explained in Chapter Four.

Examples:

"You told her my secret. I am so upset because I trusted you."

"When I see you flirting with others, I feel sick, because it makes me doubt our relationship."

"I know we depend on my income, but my job is giving me ulcers, and I can hardly breathe."

In these examples, we are sharing our reality without blaming anyone. Afterward, we can make changes that nourish our well-being, even if those around us do not comply. In the end, the only person we can effectively change, is ourselves.

The only person you can change is yourself.

We might need to end something, such as a relationship, a job, a bad habit, or a pattern of behavior. Or, we might need to begin something, such as a good habit, more education, a new job, or a healthy way to enjoy ourselves.

When we learn to control and take responsibility for our chronic outrage (biochemical or psychological), we can begin to render ourselves the aid we need to feel better.

Choose your battles.

Release the need to always be right. Sometimes we insist on arguing minor points, risking peace in our relationships, just to prove we are right. For instance, if our friend says that there are 52 states, but you know there are 50 states. Does it really matter? Is proving your friend wrong so important that you would risk making them feel stupid?

On the other hand, step up to the plate to defend yourself on important issues, such as your spouse accusing you of being unfaithful, when you have been faithful. This is a battle worth fighting. In this case, use constructive communication skills to make your stand.

Points to Remember

1. Make anger work for you not against you.

2. Take responsibility for your anger; do not blame others.

3. When angry, take productive steps to feel better.

4. To control your anger: calm down, affirm your worth, open your mind, put things in perspective, think productively, consider sharing with a neutral person, communicate constructively, then take healthy steps to feel better.

5. Choose your battles. Defend the important stuff; let the rest go.

6. Consider seeing a health care professional if you suspect a biochemical imbalance.

9
DISARM JEALOUSY

We feel jealous when we compare ourselves to others, and decide they are better than us or better off than us, in some regard. We feel inferior or cheated, even if we pretend we are fine.

Our impulse is to criticize or gossip about those who have something we want, such as looks, money, a specific person, a dazzling personality, acclaim, etc. The goal is to demean the subject of our jealousy so that we can feel superior. While jealousy is common, generally harmless, and completely human, it is a damaging emotion.

When we defeat jealousy, we:

    *avoid unnecessary upset

    *do not judgmentally compare ourselves to others

    *are more appealing

    *realize that no one is perfect, and everyone has weaknesses

    *realize our strengths are just as great as everyone else's

    *secure our self-esteem by celebrating ourselves

    *focus on and nurture what is best in us

How Jealousy Works

We largely cope with jealousy by over inflating our ego with an attitude that we are better than others, or under-inflating our ego with an attitude that we are inferior to others.

Over-inflating our Ego

It is very human to let our ego reign at one time or another in our lives, if not often. When our ego is inflated, we are saying, "See, I am important." We boast, and insinuate to others that their life experiences are inferior to ours, and that they are inferior to us. We need to feel *more* important than others, and we are proactive in accomplishing that goal.

One method is to demean and trip up the subject of our jealousy, as if somehow that will put us higher in the running. No one is allowed to be better than us. No one. Perpetuating this attitude, we keep the throne. If we are in control, we feel safe.

Interestingly, while we can sing high praise to ourselves, the criticism we dish out is not so easily digested when served up to us. We might pout or fire back with everything we've got. This can sometimes take the form of undeserved revenge.

Revenge is a desperate attempt to fling back the upset our offender incited (whether purposeful or not), and deliver a crushing blow. When successful, we have a brief feeling of superiority, before the underlying fear of inferiority again nips at our heels. Hmm, who else can we demean?

In truth, a narcissistic state of mind is not conducive to healthy relationships, and getting revenge does nothing but breed sadness in the world.

When our insecurity demeans others through excessive boasting or revenge, we don't really win. More and more, we will find ourselves alienated and alone, for people don't feel good when associating with us. Arrogance tends to repel people, especially those who have a healthy sense of self.

Under-inflating our Ego

When our ego is under-inflated, we feel inferior to those who possess what we seek in an area that is important to us, such as appearance, intelligence, financial status, achievement, or love. In feeling sorry for ourselves, we are jealous. This jealousy can manifest into destructive behaviors, such as starving ourselves, food binging, substance abuse, self-harm, or more commonly, general depression. We might even stop trying to be our ideal, and just accept that we don't measure up.

Indulging Jealousy

Whether we berate others or ourselves, we are swimming in a pool of woe. Jealousy is an ugly feeling, and perhaps why they call it the green-eyed monster. If taken to extremes, it can take us into tragedy, such as suicide or homicide.

How to Defeat Jealousy

When we judgmentally compare another's strengths to our weaknesses, we feel jealous. When we compare another's weaknesses to our strengths, we feel more secure. All this comparing is an invitation for jealousy. We are all different in a multitude of ways. It's not a competition. Just because we don't excel in certain things doesn't mean we aren't a good person or don't excel in other arenas not up for comparison at the moment. Instead of trying to shine like others, if we would shine as ourselves, we would find that we shine just as beautifully as any other, *in our own way.*

We all shine beautifully in our own way.

The minute jealousy strikes, we can nip it in the bud by acknowledging we have talents and achievements all our own, including ones the subjects of our jealousy may not. Beneath the glimmer and shine of those we envy are weakness and fears, hardship and strife.

No one can escape the labor required to sow the field of our life and reap the fruit. Whether it appears so or not, everyone struggles. It's just that we all struggle with different things and don't necessarily advertise it the world. Just because we don't see others struggle doesn't mean they don't. Their struggle might be a secret sadness that is never shared.

The wealthy person might be deeply lonely, feeling loved only for money. He or she might be tormented by being too short or too tall, or by a low I.Q, or carry deep emotional scars from childhood.

The successful person might have a secret drug problem, or have lost a child, or battled cancer. The beautiful person might associate worth with appearance, so terrified of looking old that a long future of plastic surgery lay ahead in a desperate attempt to maintain self-worth.

If we could see the whole picture of another, what we are jealous of might be all they have compared to a bounty of sorrows we do not see. Our perceptions of others are subjective and speculative. *I bet her life is perfect. All these couples look so happy. He gets everything he wants. She has it made. He is so lucky.* Even if there is some truth in our view, there will always be more to everyone that we do not perceive.

In short, the best way to sidestep jealousy is to *stop* focusing on what anyone else has or doesn't have, and focus on ourselves, not on we don't have, but on what we do.

When we celebrate our uniqueness, we begin to, in a way, fall in love with ourselves, deeply appreciating the abilities we possess and who we are as a person. To this end, ask yourself, "What do I like about me? What am I good at?" Nurture those strengths and just watch how you blossom! You might be quite surprised at what you become.

As we nourish our own abilities, we will begin to discover our purpose for living, not someone else's. Who we are meant to be is a mystery until we feed ourselves the compassion and care that we need to come into fruition. Until we give ourselves that chance, jealousy will ever be knocking at our door, crawling in through the windows, and popping up in our lives to torment us.

Defeating jealousy breeds kindness.

When we feel secure, we can be kind to those with whom we are jealous or in competition. When we show our appreciation for other individuals, we are more appealing. This is a very attractive quality, and will endear others to us. This can be done quite easily *if* we have a deep appreciation for ourselves and our *primary* focus is on beholding our own greatness. This is not conceit, but rather a profound embrace of our worth.

Points to Remember

1. When we compare ourselves to another, and feel inadequate, we are jealous.

2. The under or over-inflated ego is a product of jealousy.

3. Acting out of spite does not quell our deep down insecurity.

4. Spiting ourselves is unnecessary and misguided.

5. The subjects of our jealousy have struggles and weaknesses, whether we see them or not.

6. The solution to defeating jealousy is to focus on our own strengths and gifts.

7. Defeating jealousy breeds kindness.

10
BATTLE DEPRESSION

Depression comes easy when things don't go our way and there are no signs on the horizon that they will. Depression is a by-product of feeling hopeless and helpless. When depressed, our motivation wanes. If mild or occasional, these are the times we want to pull the cover over our heads and wait for the day to be over, but we don't. If severe, we do. We have given up, and it is too hard to get out of bed in the morning.

While depression is normal from to time to time, if we allow it to consume us, we can get sucked into substance abuse, addictions, or other destructive behaviors. Or we might just shut down and start to die.

When we battle depression in a healthy manner, we:

*do not judge ourselves

*we begin where we are at, taking small steps

*have compassion for our situation

*don't look at the past or future, only the moment

*give ourselves a chance to thrive

*incorporate good nutrition, exercise, and maybe a health
 care professional

Sometimes our depression is physiological or just too much to bear. In these cases, it is recommended to see a health care professional.

However, no matter the intensity or duration of the depression, there some simple things we can do to feel better.

1. *Focus on the moment.* Do not think of tomorrow, or the next year, or the future at all. Put the subject of the depression, such as, *I can't get a job, a mate, approval, or ahead in life,* on a shelf. At any given moment ask yourself, "What healthy thing can I do right now to help me feel better?" It might be as simple as watering the garden, seeing a movie, or visiting an old friend. It is different for everyone at every moment. Even taking a shower, or putting on soothing music can slightly alter our mind state. It is the little things that lift us slowly from our depression. Continue taking small steps in pursuit of the lighter and brighter *simple* joys.

2. *Make positive incremental changes.* Each day, or week, or month, just add one healthy thing to your diet, such as a vegetable, or salad, and cut back just a bit on unhealthy things. For example, instead of twelve donuts have eleven. This will help you slowly regain a feeling of power over your life.

Each day add a little nicety, such as watching a comedy, taking a bubble bath, listening to inspiring music, stroll around your yard and enjoy the outdoors, or spend two minutes with the stars at night. While it is difficult to do these simple things when depressed, assuming they will bring no relief, do them anyway.

In addition, each day, do a little less self-defeating behavior. For instance, instead of waving off loved ones, maybe listen to them. Instead of hiding from life, go to the zoo or a museum.

3. *Loosen your perceptions.* Sometimes our depression is fed by our idea of what is happening and why. But we can only see and know so much, and the whole truth might be out of our sight. Partial truths can be completely changed once we have a broader point of view. But sometimes we can't get it, not yet. Say to yourself, "I am just going to keep taking small steps, and eventually I will see where I am going."

Working our way out of depression is a moment by moment venture. Be open to do whatever healthy act it takes to feel better, even if that answer is unclear. Remaining open can go a long way toward receiving solutions that can truly help. Then, one day we will poke our head out of our hidey-hole and see blue sky.

4. *Move.* Another great thing we can do when depressed is to MOVE. Take a walk, hike, run, do a few jumping jacks, go swimming, play a sport. While moving is the last thing we want to do when depressed, if we can push through that block and move anyway, it can make a world of difference.

5. *Be patient.* If depression is chronic, don't worry about solving your problems. You are in a hole, begin where you are at, one tiny step at a time.

6. *Be kind to yourself.* Do not fault yourself for being depressed. It is what it is. Sometimes for whatever reason, depression is like a passage we go through, sometimes short, and sometimes long. Sometimes there is a viable reason, such as a death in the family, and sometimes it is a biochemical imbalance in our bodies that can often be altered with good health practices.

Every time you tell yourself, "Why even try; I give up." Say, "Every day is a brand new day. If I just keep putting one foot in front of the other, I will walk out of the darkness."

Points to Remember

1. Depression results when we feel hopeless, and helpless.

2. To regain control over your life, each day, make positive incremental changes and slowly decrease unhealthy behaviors.

3. Focus on the moment and know you have the power to take tiny steps toward simple joys.

4. Stay open to positive solutions not yet in your awareness.

5. Move.

6. Be patient.

7. Be kind to yourself.

11
SURVIVE ABUSE WITH DIGNITY

Abuse has many faces. Sometimes the abuser is so crafty we may not realize we are, in fact, being abused. Other times we know we are, but we hang in there anyway for one reason or another.

We all have, at some time in our lives, been mistreated, sometimes minorly and sometimes majorly. If major, often long after we are away from the abuser, we develop a kind of post-traumatic stress that keeps the bad experience alive in our present. Humiliation, anger, and shame are common culprits, all indicative of a loss of dignity.

The secret to surviving abuse that still haunts us is to reclaim our dignity. We can't change the past, but by honoring ourselves in the present, we can change how we *feel* about the past. Our dignity can't be robbed, only given up. And we can take it back.

Whether our maltreatment is a thing of the past or current, we can always champion our dignity, and our weapon is self-respect. When our self-respect is high, we do not tolerate abuse, not from others, and not even from ourselves.

We become our own hero, now and forever. Even if an unsavory event should occur, we can keep our dignity, our power, and our self intact. It is a state of mind.

This state of mind can help us make needed stands, remove ourselves from bad situations, sever unhealthy relationships, and most of all, ensure that we continue to grow in healthy ways.

When we survive abuse with dignity, we:

    *can champion ourselves

    *do not fixate on the past, nor fear the future

*improve our current life situation

*give no energy to those who exhibit abusive behavior

*resolve to never invite or tolerate abuse

*resolve to keep our honor and self-esteem high, always

Handling Abusive People

Sometimes love for our abusers is what keeps us there. We make excuses for them because we understand their pain. We might be fed promises or apologies if we continue the relationship. We might keep hoping they will change. However, when we need someone we care about to change their abusive behavior, we must first change the way we feel about ourselves.

When we begin to champion our dignity with self-respect, we are no longer willing to enable others to abuse us or convince us we deserve punishment. We make a stand and will not be fodder to their blaming rationalizations.

If those treating us poorly are important relationships, championing our dignity with self-respect will set a precedent that if they want to keep and or improve the relationship, they must treat us with decency. We will not be shamed, no matter what they say or do. Those abusers who are capable of honoring us will begin the process of self-examination and healthier behavior, and perhaps save the relationship.

Many abusers, however, are not capable of honoring us because deep down they do not honor themselves. They do not want to change. They like things as they are. People who do not want to change abusive behavior will blame those around them for everything in their lives that are going wrong.

In these cases, and in those where safety is a concern, consider severing the relationship in the safest and smartest way possible. This might involve seeking psychological advice, a shelter, and/or the law. In most cases, the abusers will then seek out less well-adjusted targets to torment.

Promises from chronic abusers mean nothing. Until a healthy

change in the abuser is demonstrated over time, perhaps through therapy or a definitive and visible prolonged change in their lifestyle, we can honor ourselves and live a full life without them.

We can always choose with whom we want to relate, even if it doesn't seem like it. We are free to decide. This is true of even those who pose no real threat, but cause us stress. We don't *have* to relate with those that rub us the wrong way. We can live our lives in whatever manner is healthiest for us as an individual. That is our right.

Self-Abuse

Sometimes we demean ourselves by going to great lengths to attain another's approval. We might suppress our true self, or circle around someone like he or she is the center of the universe. We then are making them more important than us. This is a form of self-abuse. We need that person's approval to approve of ourselves. If we instead champion our dignity with self-respect, we can release the *need* for anyone's approval, (even though it is quite pleasant to have), and instead celebrate ourselves. It is a wonderful feeling to spread our metaphorical wings and honor our own great worth.

When we honor ourselves, old wounds from our past abuse begin to heal, current abuse ends, and future abuse is obsolete. Our honor shines through in any situation, and overrides those who maltreat us. There is great power in keeping our dignity, and behaving in ways that exude self-respect, despite opposition. In the end, even if we are disliked for our show of strength, we are still respected, most of all by ourselves.

Surviving abuse with dignity includes a number of constructive behaviors, depending on the setting and relationship.

Abuse in the Workplace

Possible responses are:

1. Set boundaries of what you are willing to do and not do.

2. Toot your horn to your boss.

3. Ask for a raise.

4. Don't expend energy to the point of self-abuse.

5. Seek a new job.

Abuse from a Mate

Possible responses are:

1. Don't waste energy arguing. State the situation that is upsetting you in a respectful way. For example, "When you treat me this way, I don't feel respected." If your partner's response to your communication is combative, you can say something like, "When you talk to me like that, I feel invalidated."

2. If communicating, even constructively, proves to ignite arguments every time, stop trying. Focus on your own life and how you can improve it.

3. If you don't feel respected at any given time, depending on the person, share or don't share, but always remove yourself from that person or situation and go do something you enjoy.

4. If afraid, quietly, respectfully, smartly, and safely, remove yourself from the relationship.

Abuse from your Child

Possible responses are:

1. Use constructive communication to share your upset. If your child gets mad and responds with abusive comments, shift into listening and summarizing what she is saying. This can help you see either the root cause of your child's anger, or help your child see how unreasonable she is being.

2. If your child acts unappreciative, remain loving, but do less for him. If your child complains you are doing less, respond with something like, "Well, I am worn out doing all that stuff for you, so I need to take care of myself by doing more stuff for me."

3. If your child treats you poorly, remain loving, put more energy into taking care of yourself. If your child complains, for example,

that she's mad because you won't take her to the movies, respond with something like, "Well, I am upset about the way I was treated earlier, and I don't feel like taking you to the movies."

Self-respect is a neutral energy.

Self-respect is a neutral energy. We neither take nor give abuse. We give neither positive or negative energy to those who don't treat us well. For instance, we don't try to please them, nor do we try to hurt them. We don't act afraid, nor do we taunt them. We simply take care of ourselves. People can do what they will, but that doesn't mean we have to engage or even be around it.

If we remain neutral
those mistreating us receive no energy
to fuel their ill-behavior.

We each have a story to unfold, and an adventure to be had. Every person and every story is equal in greatness and worth. But when we honor our own story instead of being the victim in someone else's, and champion our dignity instead of giving it away, we not only avoid the sting of abuse, but we open doors to a positive future.

Points to Remember

1. The more we respect ourselves, the less we can be mistreated.

2. Abusive people do not want to change, but prefer to transfer their pain onto others.

3. When we claim our dignity now, we can change the way we feel about the past.

4. Acting out of self-respect will guide us out of any abusive circumstance.

5. We can feel our dignity no matter what has happened to us.

12
TURN TRAUMA INTO TRIUMPH

All trauma is healthily met by undergoing a period of grief. Sometimes we are not ready to grieve right away, and sometimes we are.

When we aren't, it is often because we are in shock and need time to realize this 'thing' actually happened. If we go too long staving off or sedating our grief, our raw emotion will eventually burst out, often destructively. We might lash out at others, ourselves, be derelict in our responsibilities, or neglect our loved ones. We might even turn our grief into grudges with those around us, or a vendetta against those who hurt us. Any form of anger in these cases, is coming from pain. So again, until the pain is felt and grieving is had, our lives cannot get back on a healthy track.

Once the grieving begins, we are on the road to recovery. We may cry, scream, retreat, and reach out to others, for a while. A while is a different length for each individual. Grieving is part of processing the pain. We might replay the event over and over, thinking of ways it could have been prevented. We might feel responsible, or that others were, and harvest anger toward any who we feel played a part in the traumatic occurrence. After pushing past that, we can move beyond grieving and find constructive ways to move on.

When we turn trauma into triumph, we:

  *allow ourselves to feel the pain and go through the grieving process

  *realize that if we were responsible, we can learn from the trauma and do better

  *realize that if we were not responsible, that others were doing the best they could at that given time, even if the behavior was unsavory

*take the experience and use it to better our lives or the lives of others.

Getting Stuck in Emotional Pain

Replaying trauma in our minds for a while is natural. Trying out blame, guilt, and hate is also normal for a bit. It is part of the healing process. But if we hold on too long in the replay and the emotions involved, we become cemented in a torment we cannot shake. In essence, we create a living hell for ourselves.

When we cling to our pain, we are choosing to believe our interpretation of the event, blocking out the full picture.

Example: Our interpretation of being rejected by our romantic partner, might be: *My lover dumped me*. A fuller picture would broaden that perspective. For instance, *Yes, I was dumped by my lover, but that doesn't make him or her scum; it simply means that either we were not a right match for each other, or one or both of us have emotional baggage that is being used to blame the other.*

Or if in ending a bad relationship, we might conclude, *My mate never loved me*. The fuller picture might be that maybe our mate did love us, but he or she was so emotionally stunted that expressing it was too difficult. Yet, in clinging to our initial belief that our lover dumped us, we perpetuate the trauma.

In the instance of infidelity, we might replay our conclusion, *He or she betrayed us, and we will never forgive*. The bigger picture might be that maybe our mate did turn against us, but the reason involved a desperate attempt to cope with inner torment, even though a line was crossed. On the other side, the cheating might be rationalized as I *was being neglected, or I didn't feel loved.* Because the root of the suffering is not addressed, the cheating behavior will likely continue with the current or future mate. Yet, in both instances, seeing only the tip of the iceberg and not what lies beneath, will perpetuate these behaviors and continue to stir trauma. Sustaining this is what lies beneath the iceberg: age-old anger, fear, and pain being relived in the present.

In the event of an accident that caused harm or death, we might get stuck in a loop of blaming, or if only's. But the bigger picture is that at the time of the occurrence, there was no forward vision of what was about to happen. At that moment everyone involved was thinking, feeling, and doing the best they could without realizing the folly about to occur. We are all moving along in our personal evolution at different paces and different phases. We just grow as we grow. Even as we grow into age until we die, we too are always growing on the inside.

Down the line we can observe our past behavior and see the folly in it, but at the time, given all the variables in our lives that we have forgotten, we did what we could, in our semi-blindness to reality, in order to cope, survive, and thrive. And so does everyone else.

Yet, out of every hardship, great growth and beauty can be had if and when we are ready to move on. In keeping with this line of thought, to break out of our stuck place, ask, "How can I grow from this? How can I become a better person or make the world a better place *because* of this experience?

If we should feel somehow responsible, at least in part, this thinking can help us forgive ourselves. If a loved one was hurt by this horrible event, then honor that person by turning the whole thing into productive action.

For example, if a loved one who always encouraged us to step out of our comfort zone to improve our life has been killed and we feel responsible, we can honor that person by taking that uncomfortable step.

If we accidentally left our pet in the car and it died, we can make a vow that we will always double check our car for any living creatures before we leave it, and share what happened with others so they don't have our experience. In this, we might save countless others, and perhaps have even deferred a more horrific incident in our own future.

In the case of being victimized, we can use that to take positive steps to deterring that event from ever happening again. If we can become stronger and wiser for anything that has happened to us, then it is not in vain.

We have the power to heal from trauma, always. It is not what happens to us, it is what we do with what happens to us.

> *It is not what happens to us,*
> *it is what we do*
> *with what happens to us.*

Often it is the sleep hours that are the most difficult because we have no distractions. We are just sitting there quietly with our gaping wound.

Simple techniques to help relieve emotional pain:

1. Before bed, release painful thoughts and feelings and replace them with thoughts such as these:

I will get through this, and come out stronger.

I will grow from this.

I will make something good of this.

I will learn from this, and do better.

I forgive myself, for at the time, I was doing the best I could.

I forgive others, because at that time, they were doing the best they could.

2. During the day, take extra loving care of yourself. Movement is very healing. A nice walk or jog, or a little yoga or tai chi can be most helpful.

3. Find positive or creative ways to express yourself, such as: sharing with others what is going on inside you; write your feelings in a poem, song, or journal; sing along with songs that help you vent; express your feelings through art, either by doing it or displaying posters, sculptures, or pictures that help you feel better.

4. Commune with nature or your belief in a higher power.

5. Let yourself cry from time to time. Even screaming into a pillow can be helpful. Often, getting out the deep down pain is

highly cathartic. Then literally hug yourself and say, "I can make something good of this."

When expressed enough, the sting of the event has a way lessening. Let your motto be, "I will be okay. I will make the most of my life."

Believe in yourself.

Emotional pain is a highly powerful catalyst for untold good or further horror. We all have powerful abilities. Until we are tested, we cannot begin to know the extent of our own greatness. When trauma hits, it is a profound opportunity to find out.

The path we choose is up to us. This is a decision that we make, and only we can make it. Either we decide to hold onto the pain, or we decide to let it go and rise from the ashes into something better.

We can rise from the ashes into something better.

When we hold on to the pain, the feelings evoked from bad memories, sustained by our mere interpretation of them, become weights that pull us under. When enough is enough, it can be helpful to imagine putting our painful memories on a harbored ship. Then cut the ties and see the ship sailing away into the distance until it disappears. Then focus on the present and make it better.

If we just don't want to or can't seem to turn things around, seeking the right mental health professional can make a phenomenal difference. When we do this, we are admitting we are in trouble and we want with all our hearts to have a better life. Find the right therapist for you. It is okay to *interview them*, or try a few.

The road to recovery is best expedited when we keep our eye on the ball of growing into all we can be right now.

Points to Remember

1. Take time to grieve and express pain.

2. Stop blaming self or others and accept that everyone was doing their best at that time in their lives.

3. Move

4. Commune with nature.

5. Use every trauma as an incentive for personal growth, and as an opportunity to help or educate others.

6. Appreciate what you do have, including the people in your life.

7. We can all rise from the ashes and make our lives more than they would have been without the trauma.

Modalities that Empower

13
OPEN YOUR MIND

We humans often close our minds to anything outside our current belief system, especially in this day and age. With the advance of communications technology, we have become globally connected, exposed to countless beliefs, ideas, and perceptions. We are bombarded with a preponderance of stimuli from a variety of communication sources that can leave us overwhelmed, confused, and a little afraid. To stay sane, we must decide what to believe. These beliefs anchor us from getting lost in a storm of ideas, and give us stability, security, and a life direction.

We generally choose to believe what suits us best at any given time. Our choices are made based on what gives *meaning* to us. Our environment, culture, and personality will help shape those decisions. Yet, what we choose to believe is not necessarily what is, or all that is.

While some of us remain open-minded to tweak or change our beliefs, many of us lock the door and throw away the key, rejecting all views outside our own. No amount of logic can change our minds. We cannot be dissuaded. In this, our world can become quite small, disconnected from other positive people and experiences, shutting out new and possibly advantageous information that could potentially better our lives.

Our restricted point of view is limited and limiting. While every point of view has validity, no one point can corner the market on all reality. If we are content in our small world, there is nothing wrong with that. Even so, the light of truth has a way of seeping through the cracks, eventually. This might conflict with what we *want* to believe. For instance, we believe our children must follow a certain path, so we push them into it with everything we've got. Yet, they are unhappy and our relationship with them suffers because we cannot, will not, see things from their point of view.

Opening our minds does not mean we must never settle on a belief. We must have a foundation of beliefs to use as a launch pad for living. However, remaining open-minded allows us to alter or expand our beliefs, enriching our life experience. Like changing a camera lens from close up to panoramic, we can more clearly see the world around us, and our potential place in it.

Each time we accept new information to be valid, it changes the big picture a little, or maybe a lot. In seeing more of the big picture, we often change our attitude, and hence make better choices that change the way we experience life.

When we open our minds, we:

   *have clearer and truer understandings

   *have more information, and a broader view of reality

   *have more choices and can try new things

   *are more tolerant and less judgmental

   *get along better with others

   *are less likely to get in a rut

   *facilitate personal growth

   *more excited to live

We cement beliefs to maintain our chosen reality.

We humans, at some time or another, go through varying degrees of defending our beliefs, and discounting all others. This doesn't mean we are bad, or wrong. It just means we aren't ready to move on to the next stage of our development. To remain, we must harbor stubbornly held opinions that anchor us to our chosen reality. Example: *I am a victim and it's everyone else's fault!*

This particular belief maintains a reality that we are helpless, and cannot save ourselves. We then manipulate others to do the job. But we always need more because we won't do anything to save ourselves. This creates a lot of drama in our relationships. We're happy if people give us their kindly attention, and bitter if they won't, or get tired of doing it. When that happens, we then confirm our belief. *I am a victim, and it's all your fault!*

When we stubbornly defend our selected beliefs to the *exclusion* of all else, we are trying to convince ourselves that we are right and therefore safe in our *chosen* reality. Stuck in our cocoon, we impede our ability to grow as a person.

Growing as a person can be scary because we don't know what will happen if we change our behavior. We feel somewhat secure in our little world. And until we are ready, we aren't coming out.

Sometimes anger is the guard at the gate, keeping us in a dungeon of dark emotions. We can't see the good in life, but rather go around and around on our wheel of bitterness. The wheel might be something like, *I hate him for what he did to me, and now my heart is closed.* Or, *I was abused and now my life is ruined.* Or, *I made a poor choice and I deserve to be punished.* This then becomes our spotlight and our minds are closed to any positive future.

When we have had enough and can't take it anymore, we generally either go down the drain and die, or set our minds to climb out of our fond, but upsetting reality. If we choose to survive, our mind opens to new ideas that can render positive solutions. We then begin to grow out of our small world.

For instance, the perpetual victim takes steps to rescue herself. The more self-sufficient she becomes, the more she sees others were not as bad as she believed them to be. She now realizes that she has the power to overcome anything with flying colors.

So often, and many years after the fact, we begin to see the other side of things. This is called personal growth. And personal growth requires an open mind.

Mind Opening Technique

Add the word maybe to all conclusions, such as:

I know she hates me . . . maybe.

I know I am right. . . maybe.

I know he did it . . . maybe.

The earth is on the brink of destruction . . . maybe.

I can't do this . . . maybe.

He can be trusted . . . maybe.

This is a good investment . . . maybe.

You are wrong! . . . maybe.

An open mind is a flexible mind.

Be flexible. If what you are doing isn't working, try something else. The ability to be flexible and respond differently if our actions either stalemate or worsen our lives, is response ability. The ability to respond in different ways. Responsibility.

Clinging to stubbornly held conclusions digs us into a hole, alienating us from so much and so many. We might align only with those who believe as we do, and thus lose out on many precious relationships. And the ones we do have . . . often suffer.

When we are flexible, we not only have a better chance of fostering positive relationships, but we can also shift gears if necessary to better our situation. *I thought I was right, but maybe I jumped to a conclusion.*

By simply adopting a flexible attitude, we can stop ourselves from looping unsavory life experiences like a record that never changes its tune.

When we bend with the winds of our lives, we are less liable to break, and more likely to survive the storm with our honor and dignity intact.

An open-minded attitude would be:

I will proceed with a certain set of beliefs that seem to currently serve me. However, if my well-being begins to suffer, I will reassess and be open to change.

Sometimes we know there is more to a story than what we believe, but for whatever reason, for now, we just need to believe it. That's okay! When the time for change comes, you will know it.

Points to Remember

1. Our minds close when we cement the beliefs we currently *need* to feel secure.

2. When we close our minds, we cheat ourselves of the knowledge needed to stimulate personal growth.

3. When we cling to our own view to the exclusion of all others, we create distance in our relationships.

4. Sometimes we have to play out the reality our beliefs hold in place until we can't take it anymore.

5. When we broaden our view, we can integrate new ideas into our current belief system.

6. When we open our minds, we experience greater unity with those outside our social circle.

7. An open mind is a flexible mind, enabling us to try different things to attain desired results.

8. When we can bend with the wind, we are less likely to break.

14
TEMPER JUDGEMENT

Hand in hand with keeping an open mind is tempering our judgments.

Yes, we need to make judgments based on available information in order to know how we should proceed with our lives. However, allowing fluidity in our judgments, subject to new information, keeps us from creating future problems for ourselves.

Our ideas are always valid, yet there is always more to everyone and everything than can be wholly understood. Since our interpretations are based on our point of view, our judgments, whether positive or negative, are discriminatory.

When we temper judgment, we:

* are open to the idea that what looks good may not be good

* are open to the idea that what looks bad might be good

* do not judge others unfavorably if they disagree with us

* have no need to gossip

* do not criticize those outside our circle whose opinions differ

*are immune to mob mentality that acts on the group consensus instead of thinking for ourselves

Judging Others.

These pesky judgments of ours (our opinions) can get us into trouble when we make them our stronghold. Making an open-minded judgment, such as *I have a bad feeling about this, so I am going to keep my distance. I could be wrong but I don't want to take a chance,* is one thing. Blackballing that person from a social group in close-minded judgment would be quite another, especially if we are wrong.

When judging others, rather than acting on our opinions, we would fair better to take our own pulse on what *effect* that person has on us. No matter what the reason, we feel how we feel around that person. Does that person catalyze personal growth and genuineness in us? Or does that person's presence make our stomach churn or our heart hurt? No matter what the truth of that person, that is less important than our reaction to being around that person. Taking that into consideration, we can decide for ourselves how much, little, or no involvement we choose to have with anyone, based solely on how we feel around that person.

> *How we feel around a person*
> *is more telling than*
> *what we believe to be true about that person.*

We might decide at a later date that we felt uncomfortable around someone because we were jealous, or he or she triggered an unsavory emotion from our past, but was in fact, innocent in intention. Even so, stepping back until the waters clear can be extremely beneficial in hindering unnecessary drama.

Sometimes we judge others harshly because we do not want to look at ourselves. In casting blame, we are always innocent and excused from looking our own inner monster in the eye.

Sometimes we judge others the way we judge ourselves. If we would never think of having an affair, we would likely judge others harshly who do. If we have had an affair, we would likely be less judgmental on those who confide the same.

We also often judge our role in life and cast supporting roles to those around us. For example, if we judge ourselves a victim, we will see life through victim glasses. We are likely then to view others as villains, even if they are not. Along this same line, if we judge ourselves a hero, we are likely to see others as victims, even if they are doing all right.

Sometimes we judge others negatively to boost our own ego. Gossip falls into this category. If we can get others to agree on our negative perception of another, we tend to feel superior.

No matter how or why we judge others negatively, it is anti-productive. Changing this behavior begins with a productive thought such as, *I have an idea about this person or situation, but there is always more to every person, and every situation that meets the eye. Who am I to judge?*

We don't like being judged, and neither does anyone else. However, if we slip, and it is common and normal that we do, chalk it up as an attempt to secure our own worth.

Being Judged.

Being human, most of us react strongly to being judged, especially when we are misjudged. When we are wrongly judged and react with extreme upset, it is a sign that we need to be more comfortable in our own skin. In the course of our lives we all will be wrongly and negatively judged by many, even if we are generally beloved. People's judgments of us are just that, an unsubstantiated point of view that is a reflection of the judges, not the judged.

> *Other people's judgments of us*
> *are filtered through their point of view,*
> *and thus subject to error.*

We can deflect these undue judgments with a simple motto:

No matter what anyone says or does to me, I am always worthy.

Judging Ourselves

We tend to judge ourselves by how we *believe* others view us. When we *think* others judge us negatively, we often feel the sting, even if they aren't. And if they are, we can only feel bad if some part of us agrees that those negative judgments are true. Example: *They are right; I'm not good enough.* If we do not concur, we remain relatively unaffected. Example: *They don't know what they are talking about; I'm more than good enough.*

Remember, no one knows us better than we know us, and even if the feedback we get holds elements of truth, this is no reason to demean ourselves. As previously discussed, our worth is intrinsic and cannot be altered, no matter what. We all fall short of any given social world's view of perfection. Every human being on earth has room for self-improvement and personal growth, always. This is a great thing, not a bad one.

In judging ourselves harshly, we often fixate on a binocular view of an event, or events, excluding the larger picture of our lives, which would include many wonderful things we have done. It would also encompass our whole life history and hundreds of variables that made us what we are today. If we saw it all at once, we would understand the root of all our behaviors and feel quite sympathetic to all we have endured.

However, as we do not see all this, we sometimes judge ourselves harshly. The lower our self-esteem, the more we will block out what is good in us, and reinforce our low self-opinion.

While we cannot really understand ourselves completely, we can *feel* our true selves deep within. When our emotion is sparked, and we feel inspired, such as being moved by the stars, or fairy tales, science, or art, we come to know our true self. Only we can know this. Others can conjecture, and judge, but only in themselves can they find *their* truth, not *the* truth. *If* feeling wrongly judged, think, *Others can believe whatever they want of me; I know who I am.*

This doesn't mean we can't make a statement of truth to set the record straight and nobly defend ourselves. This may or may not alter the opinion of the judger. Some people *need* to maintain negative opinions of others in order to like themselves. In these cases, a noble stand to set the record straight is to make *us* feel better, getting it off our chest, and to boost our self-esteem.

Points to Remember

1. Judging others negatively is an attempt to feel secure, which causes friction in relationships.

2. Our subjective judgments lack full insight into the whole story of any person or circumstance.

3. How we feel around another is more telling than what we believe to be true about that person.

4. Other people's judgments of us are filtered through their point of view, and thus subject to error.

5. When judged unfavorably, realize that the judgment is more a reflection of the judger than the judged.

6. Judging others by the standard we hold for ourselves, can be short-sighted.

7. When we judge ourselves by how we *think* others view us, we short-change our true self.

8. The more secure we are within, the less need we have to judge ourselves or others.

15
LOVE YOUR BODY

Love your body. Love your body. Love your body. Our body is our best friend. It gets us around, gives us thoughts, emotions, senses, and an adventure to be had. Our body is always talking to us, letting us know if something is wrong or right. Our body talks to us by feeling hungry or thirsty, ill or nervous, hot or cold, pain or pleasure. It warns us of danger, such as hairs standing up on the back of our neck, or makes us feel good, such as an open warm feeling in our heart.

When we treat our body right, it treats us right, and without it, well, where would we be? However, in this crazy highly stimulating world, it is easy to forget about our bodies until they begin ailing. Or, we might lend more attention to how they look than keeping them healthy.

While it is human and even just animal behavior to bring attention to our bodies to attract a mate or to attain community approval, we have lures that other mammal's do not. Our mass media pounds messages subliminally and outright into our brains every day. These messages often benefit the sender, far more than the receiver.

In general, we don't know the full extent of why, for example, we want to be skinny as a rail, or eat those unhealthy foods, or to have the fashion fad of the moment, or a youthful face forever, but we do.

Adhering to these messages, we often lose touch with what is in our body's best interest. Since we live in our bodies, that poses risks.

When we love our bodies, we:

    *eat foods that make us healthy

*make health more important than a socially desired image

*calm emotions that make our bodies ill

*productively deal with stress rather than endure it

*listen to what our bodies are telling us

*are a part of our health professional's decision making

Nourishing our Bodies

We get out of our bodies what we put into them. Like animals and plants, our bodies need sunshine, fresh air, clean water, nutritious food, and movement (plants move all the time, often toward the sun).

In this day and age, we often sit at our computer, social media, or gaming device for hours on end, never seeing the sun, or giving our bodies the movement they need to stay healthy. In our fast-paced world we often consume foods that are quick and convenient at home or out, unaware of, or not caring what is in what we eat. However, when we tend our bodies with respectful commitment, we are reciprocated in kind with a healthier vehicle to give us a more vibrant life. When our bodies are treated as our very best friend, we grow amazingly healthy.

Make your body your best friend.

While the body often seems to have a mind of its own, wanting to do or not do, despite what is healthy, (a case of beer a day, donuts every morning, snacking all night long, staying sedentary most of the time, etc.), if we work compassionately with our bodies unhealthy urges, we can begin to compromise and work slowly and steadily toward a healthy outcome.

Taming Unhealthy Urges

1. *Add something healthy, and decrease something unhealthy.*

Add one healthy thing to your daily regime, such as a healthy food, or a walk, or a few sit-ups. *Decrease something unhealthy.* Decrease one unhealthy thing in your daily regime, such as instead of a pack of cigarettes, have three quarters of a pack (unless advised differently by your health care professional).

Once this becomes habit and you begin to feel better, it will be easier to add another healthy thing to your daily regime and decrease another unhealthy thing.

Unless otherwise advised by a medical professional, if slowly increasing healthy choices and decreasing unhealthy ones, positive outcomes are imminent for life.

2. *Take frequent breaks.* Take frequent breaks from sitting too long, to move and stimulate your body. It's like giving your body time out of the corral. Even moving to take out the garbage or water the plants is helpful. Running in place for one minute can do wonders. Exercise in a way that is conducive to who you are. Going to the gym is not for everyone. Sometimes walking fast down the block, playing ball with your child, or going on a hike, is a better ticket for us.

3. *Diet for life.* Find what makes *your* body feel healthier, rather than adhering to fad diets as a first resort. For instance, for many of us, the last thing we want are vegetables, but for most (unless ill advised by a health care professional) vegetables really do make us feel better. In this instance, by adding vegetables to our diet, we will eventually crave them, and the very thought of the more unhealthy foods will feel far less appealing. This then becomes a part of our very welcomed lifetime diet.

4. *Replace bad habits with good habits.* Bad habits are anything that cause you harm. Good habits are anything that make you healthier.

How to Stop Bad Habits

When we are not ready to give up a bad habit, we often rationalize why it is all right to keep. This doesn't make us bad, just human. Our bodies have been trained to use that bad habit as a band-aid for underlying stress.

Often we know, deep down, we want to break bad habits to improve our life, but we feel we *need* what we would have to give up to get through the day. Stopping a bad habit that we use to comfort ourselves cold turkey with nothing to replace it, can make us feel like we are going to die. The urgency to have what we seek to give up, can intensify. The solution is to replace bad habits with new and healthier rewards.

Replace bad habits with new and healthy rewards.

Even if the habit doesn't seem to affect our bodies, stressors that go with the habit, do. For example, gambling our money away and not being able to pay the bills. The consequences of our bad habits can cause prolonged stress to our bodies, breaking down our resistance to disease, raising our blood pressure, which makes us subject to heart attack or stroke, or negatively affecting our mental and physical health in a myriad of other ways.

With a few simple steps, we can successfully modify our bad habit.

1. *Inform yourself.* Get more informed with how the bad habits are affecting your physical, mental, and emotional worlds. This requires courage to look at the truth. How are these habits hurting you?

For example, in the case of drug addiction, get graphically informed on what the drug does to your body, and the consequence of prolonged use. Take a hard look at what else it is doing to other areas of your life.

Another example would be, in the case of pleasure spending leading to unpaid bills, thoroughly study your financial situation.

2. *Replace bad habits with good habits.* Find pleasant, healthy things to replace the bad habit, gradually or outright. If gradual, an example would be: instead of having three drinks a day, have two and a cookie to replace the third drink. If cookies eventually replace alcohol, you can work on another replacement, such as a tasty health food cookie for the more sugary ones. Or, if gambling at a casino, resulting in deep debt, is your thing, get a poker game

at home going instead (don't play for money, or have a low reasonable limit that cannot be exceeded), and take up an enjoyable hobby.

If replacing a bad habit outright, such as chronically overspending on shopping sprees, then follow some other unlived passions, such as learning to play the piano, writing that book, painting that picture, joining that hiking club, or community sports team. Do whatever uplifts you in a healthy manner.

If your bad habit is a severe addiction, life threatening, illegal, or so destructive your life is falling apart, consider professional help along with finding a variety of healthy things to comfort you, and keep yourself busy with them. Don't focus on, *oh I want this or that, I need this or that, I don't care what happens.* But rather, *I can't wait to paint, or jog, or get that class so I can learn about this or that, or go to that movie,* etc.

Bad habits are a focus. As we learn to change the channel to healthier means of comfort, feeling better snowballs on itself. We want more of whatever makes us feel happier, healthier, and in control of our lives.

The main goal is to give our body all it needs to be in tiptop shape to better all aspects of our life, and that includes removing unnecessary stressors.

Listen to your body.

Our bodies are always trying to communicate with us, if only we will listen. Physical and psychological ailments are our body's way of telling us that something is off balance. One way of discovering what is right for our bodies is to listen *less* to general information, such as this food or that drug is good or bad for our health, and pay more attention to how foods, drugs, or anything else affects *your* mental, emotional, and physical health.

In short, participate in your own healing by not blindly taking the word of anyone, and that includes health care professionals. Get second and third opinions, and put your own opinion in the mix. Health professionals are human, and can err, just as can anyone.

Make yourself part of the team.

Physical Image

Dissatisfaction with our bodies is a reaction to the social mores of any given culture in various periods of time. Sometimes the wish to achieve a desired image comes at a grave price, resulting in bodily damage, psychological eating disorders, botched plastic surgeries, exercise injuries, and a reliance on the superficial to attain and sustain self-esteem. In short, we commonly abuse our bodies to be loved.

When our bodies take a hit to benefit a desired image, we might want to rethink our priorities.

By reversing the priority of image over health to health over image, we find our image improves naturally when we feel physically, mentally, and emotionally healthy.

Further, if we could entertain the idea that the most powerful beauty cannot be contrived, but is generated from deep inside our being, we would feel empowered. What makes us beautiful is what we emanate. It is our personality, how we relate with others and the world. Think of those whom you love the most. Is it due to looks? Or who they are as a human being? Think of whom you are most devoted, to a socially pleasing body, or one whose warmth and individuality incites the deepest appreciation.

We develop an attraction to the physical appearance of those with whom we are enamored. We can be in love with all shapes and sizes. It is only commercialism that says we can't.

Shining confidence and joy attracts far more people to us than a body that reflects what social media portrays as ideal. When we have distaste for our bodies, our *attitude* is what repels people, not our bodies. Think of an actor who has played many different personalities. Which personality attracted you more to that actor? Was it the bumbling scaredy cat, or the relaxed self-confident one? How we behave is absolutely key to how attractive we appear. Emanating confidence and shining our strengths is seductively appealing.

We are attractive
when we emanate confidence
and shine our strengths.

Everybody is unique and has many gifts to offer *despite perceived flaws*. As cliché as it may seem, beauty comes from within.

There is nothing wrong in enhancing our image and being artistic with our bodies. In fact, it can be quite healthy, fun, and normal as long as it does not compromise our health.

A very easy way to stay on track is to ask yourself, "Is this action to improve my appearance going to put my body at risk? And if so, how much?"

When we abuse our bodies, it is often a reflection of unrest within us. Given this, if we are at peace with ourselves, it is easier to eat healthy and exercise moderately, get some fresh air and sun, and touch the natural world, which is healing for our spirit.

Points to Remember:

1. Make your body your best friend.

2. We get out of our bodies what we put into them.

3. Replace bad habits with good ones.

4. Listen to your body and be proactive in your own healing.

5. Choose the health care professional that is right for you, and don't be afraid to get second and third opinions.

6. Put health over body image.

7. Attractiveness comes primarily from emanating confidence, and shining our strengths.

16
REGULATE YOUR ENERGY

Our energy is going out to everything under the sun. Every time we interact with another, energy is used. Maintaining our bodies, homes, jobs, health, and relationships, takes energy.

Even thinking takes energy. We humans are prone to over analyze, generate worrisome thoughts, and replay painful memories, all of which heighten our stress.

We often tell ourselves we must do certain things on our mental list, even if we are exhausted. If we succeed, we usually feel run down. If we do not, we tend to generate more stress and perhaps give ourselves a mental beating.

Or, we might go the other way and procrastinate, overwhelmed with what we have to do. We might even try to manipulate others to do the work we know is ours. This can result in a rather sluggish, *I don't care*, attitude, leaving us feeling unfulfilled and rather incapable. This spills out into our relationships and can cause a whole different kind of conflict.

Regulating our energy is of prime importance if we are to maintain our mental, emotional, and physical health.

When we regulate our energy, we:

   *expend energy in ways that keep us physically, emotionally, and mentally healthy

   *make our first priority, kindness to ourselves and others

   *replenish ourselves if we feel depleted, no matter who or what is put on the backburner

   *give positive attention to others if we claim center stage too often

   *do more for others if we notice they are doing more for us

*are healthier and happier, enjoying what we have and the people in our lives

When we fail to regulate our energy, it is generally because we are giving too much and taking too little, or giving too little and taking too much.

Giving Too Much. Taking Too Little

Martyrs and Nurturers

Those of us with strong martyr and/or nurturing tendencies often give more energy than received, taking greater care of others than necessary, and sacrificing more for others than we should. While giving, nurturing, and sacrifice can be beautiful, when overdone, it has a way of back firing.

This chronic act of giving energy without replenishing can incite illness, accidents, depression, mental breakdown, and sometimes suicide. Suicide is not always conscious. One can just be too tired and mentally give up. This propagates carelessness, which can result in fatal mistakes, such as car accidents. Or, some might feel sacrifices are necessary and become so malnourished and emaciated within, death follows.

When we give too much, we often feel taken for granted, unappreciated, sad, and maybe even lonely, because the level of care given is either not received in the way we meant it, or not returned.

In the case of showering others with nonstop attention as in gifts, compliments, or niceties, they can get overwhelmed. They might even feel a little invaded and retreat from us.

Or if we do too much for others, such as taking over their responsibilities in varying degrees, we are in fact, encouraging them to depend on us. In other words, be *dependent* on us. In this, not only do we rob them of their personal growth, but we are grooming them to expect us to keep serving them without realizing how much it is depleting us, and how much our own needs are largely unmet. When in this predicament, we might even brew a secret anger.

Yet, in both cases, it is we who created these scenarios, and we who keep our true feelings a secret. And even if we spill the beans of feeling pressured, used, or unappreciated, it is still we who chose to expend our energy this way. No one held a gun to our head.

Reversal requires a definitive action. Do less for others, and do more kindly, nourishing things for ourselves. When we focus on fulfilling our own deep down needs instead of producing results, we begin to feel happier. We also earn a deeper respect for those observing, mostly because we are respecting ourselves.

When we retreat for a while, we not only give ourselves a break, but we give others an opportunity to do things for us. Just as giving can make us feel better, well, it makes others feel better too. If in our pulling back we seem to be forgotten, it won't much matter, for we are nourishing ourselves and broadening our horizons. In doing that, we will receive new and refreshing energy.

Overachievers

Those who expend too much energy are not necessarily martyrs or strong nurturing types, but can fall into the category of overachiever.

We overachievers often end up feeling depleted. The ongoing need to accomplish things feeds our worth and gives us an emotional high. But when we keep going and going and going without relaxing and taking time to enjoy life, the only place we eventually go . . . is down.

Some of us overachieve to receive applause. We have a need to keep filling up the mantel with trophies and awards, or keep "doing" to receive constant kudos from those around us. We often set ourselves up in situations where others say, "Of course, you will win. Of course, you will succeed," not realizing what it takes for us to attain constant victory. Then we feel pressure to make it happen.

It is not uncommon for chronic overachievers, (those who achieve far more than necessary, despite feeling over worked) to eventually have a break down and simply not even be able to get out of bed.

Reversing this behavior requires a shift from seeking a feeling of accomplishment, to taking better care of ourselves, focusing on health, enjoying simple pleasures, learning how to relax and have fun, and engaging with others in a more light hearted and affectionate manner. Fundamentally, overachievers have associated their worth with achievement. Saying often, "I am worthy because I am breathing," can help change that thinking.

Feeding the Dragon

Helping each other is a great thing, and the more of it that happens, the better. However, there is a difference between helping others help themselves, and helping others to continue on with ineffective methods of coping that keep them in their current turmoil.

Those of us who tend to give too much are also in danger of becoming great enablers of the needy. Those we continually help can leave us feeling drained, topped with a headache. The needy who perpetually require us to tend them, need an energy fix to stay the same. Our helpful suggestions go on deaf ears no matter how brilliant or often we share them. Our attention is held hostage for hours and hours, days and days, sometimes months, sometimes years. We endure an outpouring of woe expressed in words that repeat themselves eternally.

Here is the bejeweled rule: *If helping another drains you, something is wrong.*

If feeling depleted when helping another, you have become the victim of an energy vampire. These energy suckers are usually wonderful people who are unaware of the toll their turmoil takes on we willing victims who look like saviors. How can they, when we don't tell them? We are ever there, a veritable feast of energy for them to feel better while we feel worse. We have invited this, largely because it makes us feel important. Yet, we are actually hurting ourselves and enabling those dependent on us to *stay the same.*

In these cases, regulating our energy means we must become less and less available in order to regenerate. There need not be a confrontation, just a weaning process. For instance, when the needy person begins to spout his or her woe, if on the phone or electronic device, consider saying something like, "Hope you feel better; I can't talk now." If face to face, consider saying something like, "I'm really tired, I need to go now." Don't get into why you have to go, just keep it simple.

If you do get cornered into explaining, just share that you feel tired and depleted and need to take care of yourself. If the person actually cares about you, he or she won't punish you for that. If attempts at punishment are made by infliction of guilt or accusation, then it is time to disconnect from that person to save yourself. The thinking, silent or verbalized is, "Sorry you feel that way, but I matter too."

Be resolute about taking care of yourself, and disconnect before you can be convinced that they need you (need your energy) to give them a *fix.* Preying on our empathy is an effective way of sucking us in. We need to get out before the sucking begins. If the needy person's energy source is cut off, it actually gives them a chance to shoulder their own problems and feel empowered when they do. Sometimes it is kinder not to be so kind. Too much rescuing can rob others of their growth. They might seek a replacement for you, but you will be out of it, and feel *much* better.

Addiction to Giving

It feels good to give. Giving can make us feel high on life. This is wonderful in moderation, but the constant search to find more ways to give and more for whom to give is indicative of an addiction to giving. We somehow have made constant giving a prerequisite to feeling worthy. This is how we get *our* fix. This not only degrades ourselves, but puts a huge strain on our energy. We are depleted, and not really helping others or endearing them to us as intended.

The Quest for Perfection

The quest for perfection is another big energy drain. We each have our own idea of what it is to be perfect. Some of us expend an exorbitant amount of energy in that pursuit. If, in our mind, we can attain it, even for a while, we decide we can like ourselves, and that others will like us, and maybe even love us too. If we all like and love us, we are safe.

When we can't meet our own expectations, we generally feel anxious and maybe even panicky. In short, when we give too much in the quest for perfection, we eventually feel burned out.

What we may not realize, is that being perfect isn't perfect. What makes people love us is not our infallibility, but our vulnerability. We all have areas of ourselves that need work, and in revealing them, especially to loved ones, we give them a great gift. To admit we have needs, and struggles, and can't do it all, gives them not only an opportunity to help us (and feel good in so doing), but they learn that they don't have to be perfect either. Release the need to be perfect. Learn to love yourself as is, ever open to naturally growing into who you are.

Learn to love yourself as is,
ever open to growing naturally
into who you are.

Ways to regulate energy when we expend too much:

1. *Priorities.* Make the first priority on your list to treat yourself and others kindly. When these two priorities are the pillars of your life, everything goes better.

Unfortunately, these two priorities often fall at the bottom of the list. We all have priorities. For some, the most important thing is to look attractive. For others it is to make money. For some, being loved is number one. Or perhaps having a clean house is of supreme importance. A common occurrence is that our well being comes way below keeping things clean, making money, and looking attractive, etc. Our well-being, so often comes at the bottom of the list because we so often feel we can only have well being if we complete the list.

Giving affection to our loved ones, amazingly, can be down on the list too. We are so busy trying to get everything done, that the dog doesn't get pet, our child doesn't get cuddled, and intimate time with our mate is just more than we can handle at the moment.

Try this:

Except for certain circumstances, put your well-being and the well-being of others first. Treat yourself well and treat others well. If you find it hard to breathe because there are twelve things you are trying to get done, then stop. You are not treating yourself well. Calm down, catch your breath, do the most important thing and do the rest in peaceful stride, and some don't do at all.

When pressed for time, and anxious to do what you feel you must, push it down on the priority list if a loved one is ailing, or a pet looks deprived, or if the plant is drooping. Comfort your loved one, love up your pet, and water the plant. In the grocery store, don't zoom ahead of the stranger heading for the cashier, or pass cars at ten miles over the speed limit, or push others aside as you run through your list of errands, like you will die if you don't. Letting common courtesy, respect, and caring precede accomplishing other things is actually the greatest accomplishment of all.

Do these things, and watch how your stress levels begin to melt away.

2. *Simplify*. When overwhelmed, do things the *easy* way, partially, or not at all. If there is something on your daily schedule that is inhibiting normal breathing, it is okay to reschedule. It is okay to decide *not* to do something. It is okay to say no to the requests of others. It is okay to change your mind. You can leave the house messy, your car unwashed, and your laundry undone. You can ask for help if there is just too much for you to do. You can have a day doing nothing. You always have every right in the world to *take care of yourself* and put everything else on hold until you feel better.

Taking too Much. Giving too Little.

When we take too much and give too little, we are overly self-focused, and not so aware of the needs of those around us. We may have even earned the label, "Insensitive to Others."

In need of constant attention, we might suck the life out of everyone around us. *Look at me. Look at me. Look at me.* We might do this by bragging, being overly needy, or just plain obsessed with indulging ourselves at the expense of others.

We are better at taking than giving. This inequity tends to throw our relationships off balance. If we don't give back and pay kindly attention to those who give it to us, we usually wind up lonely, because who wants to be around someone who makes everything all about themselves, always.

Reasons We Hog Attention

Loneliness

Sometimes we are so lonely that if anyone gives us an inch of attention, we take a mile. We don't let anyone get a word in edgewise and may even cling possessively to anyone who gives us the time of day. We are so needy for affirmation, we drink in the attention we get to feed our deep down needs.

Woe is Me

Sometimes the hook is to espouse our woes nonstop. While we might ask, "How are you?" once in a while, the conversation is quickly turned back to ourselves. Our energy reaping involves demanding attention with an air of *nobody's problem is as big as mine.*

Wonderful Me

We might go the other way and keep the center of attention by reminding everyone how great we are. When our egos get too big, we dominate the conversation with wonderful stories about ourselves, failing to notice or give credit to the good others do, or the exciting adventures they have had. In essence, we hoard our energy and enjoy getting more from others.

We might also, in an attempt to make ourselves seem worthier and more appealing than those in our lives, withhold positive attention from them. We keep them working for it, happily absorbing their energy in that pursuit. However, this methodology almost always backfires, eventually, because everyone needs positive acknowledgment now and then. Those whom we starve from affection will, almost assuredly, in time, go elsewhere to get it.

I am the Boss

We might expect others do all the work while we make the commands. We tell ourselves we are doing our part by commanding the ship, and leave the grunt work to everyone else. We exude our self-importance for commanding the situation, making ourselves the center of attention. This eventually breeds resentment and those being constantly commanded may find various ways to make their escape from us.

Let Me Save You

Sometimes we set out to save others who are not asking to be saved, nor feel that they need saving. We are actually searching for weakness in others, and aggressively throwing our energy at them. This usually makes them want to run from us, or at the very least put up a cautious wall to keep us from trespassing. Sometimes we are indulged, maybe, and if so, we may have hooked an energy sucker, which defeats our purpose.

Ways to regulate energy when we take too much:

1. Rely more on yourself to get your needs met.

2. Take responsibility for your obligations and life situation.

3. Let others talk and embrace what they say.

4. Do something nice for others, and share positive feelings toward them.

5. Ease the burden of those who do most of the work.

Personal Development

When we begin to develop the more stunted areas of our lives, and we know what those are, because we don't want much if anything to do with them, we begin to thrive, and are less dependent on others. Perhaps we rely on our mate to do all the housework, or take care of all the finances, or do all the nurturing, child rearing, or money making. We might chronically rely on our loved ones to boost our self-esteem, or need their constant attention to feel like we matter. While some of these agreements can be made in a healthy manner, often they are made because one is getting away with overall doing less, and the other is burdened with overall doing more.

The Art of Self-Nurturing

Regulating our energy in a balanced way in all cases requires an up tick in self-nurturing. Self-nurturing is about giving ourselves quiet time for deep thought, personal time for creative self-expression, time to tend our bodies with healthy food and exercise, and permission to actualize our dreams, or at least find them.

When we nurture ourselves, we pay attention to our own human struggle and give ourselves respect, compassion, and appreciation.

Nurturing ourselves means we are not martyrs. When we nurture ourselves first and keep our own cup full, it will spill over to nurture others. We can take care of ourselves *and* others.

When we are self-nurtured, we can easily say no to any who come knocking at our door for energy if we just don't have it to give.

And if we who usually take too much do have energy, maybe even in abundance, we can lend a helping hand, and caring words. We can do this, because when we have nurtured ourselves, we really don't need as much as we have taken. This is because all we have taken was an attempt to get others to feed our self-esteem. If we already have it, we can afford to be more giving to others.

When we nurture ourselves, we can more easily resist the urge to hoard our energy or take too much, or use others as a crutch to shoulder our life challenges. We want to know our own power and hence true security. Giving, when all we want to do is take, can facilitate a powerful new experience of true intimacy with other people. When all we want is positive affirmation from others, but instead share positive feelings we have toward them, with them, can bring us out of the dark and off our little island where the only person that exists is us.

Perhaps one of the most important things to remember in the fine art of self-nurturing is that, while a kind hand is always appreciated and much needed in this world, ultimately, to truly feel at our best, we must face our own dragons and pave our own way. We feel better when we know we can depend on ourselves. And believe it or not, so do others.

When we learn to regulate our energy, joy in living is substantially increased.

Points to Remember

1. Regulating our energy helps us to stay mentally, emotionally, and physically healthy.

2. The chronic act of giving energy without replenishing can lead to break down, incite illness, accidents, depression, and sometimes suicide.

3. When feeling depleted, unappreciated, or taken for granted, do less for others and more for yourself.

4. We tend to expend too much energy when feeling good depends on nurturing others, or a need to achieve, or when we carry other peoples' burdens to our detriment, overly strive toward our idea of perfection, or have a low priority to preserve our own well-being.

5. Taking too much can be a result of loneliness, self-pity, arrogance, the need to control, or to convince others they need saving.

6. If taking too much, giving more will improve all relationships.

7. Learning to nurture ourselves and tend our own well-being is the greatest step we can take in regulating our energy.

Aspirations to Live By

17
RESPECT OTHERS

We tend to respect people who share our opinions or have achieved in life what we feel is important. That respect often wanes with those who believe or behave differently. However, what is good for us is not necessarily good for everyone. Our opinions do not reign supreme over others, no matter how brilliant they may seem. While serving us, they might be disastrous for another.

We can never know another's truth. We might have a partial or pretty good idea of what would be good for them, but unless we are them, we cannot know for sure. It is for us to steer our own ship and for others to steers theirs. Just as we crash and burn in our various so-called mistakes, others also should have that privilege. That is how we learn what is right or not right for us. That is how we grow. Further, choices that might crush us, might be what another uses as a springboard to soar higher than ever before.

Supporting others in choices that seem to work for them can greatly improve the quality of our relationships. An exception might be if a loved one is on a course of self-destruction, such as drug addiction, we may need to involve professionals if possible, or at the very least lovingly voice our concern. But in the end, we all make our own choices, and if we are set on them, we cannot be stopped. We can only play it out and see what happens.

Hopefully we can survive it, learn, and grow.

When we respect others, we:

    *acknowledge that everyone has a right to their own opinion

    *realize we are all different, hence our life paths will vary

    *accept that everyone has their own way of doing things that is right for them.

    *are compassionate to those who have erred in judgment

    *are generally beloved and have healthier relationships

Respect Children

Children, being children, are in the early stages of trial and error and have further to go to realize the consequences of their choices. Yet, we often admonish and punish them, just for learning.

Of course we must monitor our children, set guidelines, and help them see the error of their ways that will work against them in life, such as hitting people when they don't get what they want.

Rather than scorch their self-esteem with hurtful words or a spanking, a more respectful alternative is to give them *natural* consequences in a loving manner. For example, they won't clean their bedroom, so don't get them that new toy they have been wanting. When they ask for it, you might say, "Well, I see your room is a mess. When I can see you are taking care of what you do have, I would be happy to get that toy for you."

It is also important to respectfully give latitude for children's developmental stages. For example, children are clumsy sometimes because they have not yet fully developed spatial ability. So, accidentally dropping that carton of eggs may not even be that they were not being careful, and yet we might accuse them of that.

In that regard, we too accidentally drop and break things now and again. It is human. If we admonish ourselves for similar acts, it is likely we were admonished for such things when we were children. Is it really necessary? Is that good for our mental health?

As our children grow older, they will fair better if we respectfully give them room to grow into who they are. For instance, a scientific type may have no interest in sports. Respect that. A little girl may hate dresses. Respect that. Whatever our child's propensity, foster it in a positive way.

Instead of encouraging our children to be socially admired, encourage them to be themselves and to do what is right, comfortable, and healthy for them as an individual.

Encourage children to grow into who they are,
not what we want them to be.

Respect Strangers

Sometimes, simple respect for strangers can yield great rewards. These tiny interactions can go a long way in making us feel better. While some strangers remain rather grumpy or detached, many more will brighten by a simple smile or a common courtesy, and thus brighten us. Sometimes these connections take us to interesting places, such as a job opportunity, or gaining a piece of information, such as a great vacation spot, that can lighten our load in life.

A word of caution: If you feel uneasy by the presence of certain people, trust that instinct and walk on by. Never give your energy to those that make your stomach turn or just give you a sick feeling. This is often an indication that that person could be dangerous, or is off balance in a way that is not in your best interest.

Believe in people.

Believing in people doesn't mean we blindly trust them. It means despite our opinions, we all have many sides to us, some quite beautiful, and some unsavory. We are complex, and more vast than we appear. People can surprise us. The ones seemingly going nowhere, out of the blue, can rise from the dregs and take a meaningful life direction. And some that seem to have everything, suddenly go down hill on a path of self-destruction.

We just don't know what is truly right for anyone at any given time. Sometimes we have to fail or be dying before we can find or choose our life direction. In short, it is often the rougher paths that lead to a brighter future. We all have the makings to create miracles in our own life, and interestingly this often happens when we are sitting in a mess.

Believing in people helps them shift their mental focus to the best of themselves. This can be quite empowering and inspire greatness. We all want to be believed in. In a way, it proves we exist.

Micromanaging Others

We don't like it when others tell us how we must live, and they don't like it when we tell them how they must live.

When we try to micromanage the lives others, we rob them of their journey toward fruition. It is akin to dictating to the oak tree, it must be an apple tree, and giving it orders on how to grow.

There are many ways of doing things. We all have our own way. For some, doing homework must be in silence, others need music, or television in the background. Some need a period of time to relax after school or work. Others like to dig in to complete tasks and rest later. Some need to do things in a traditional way, and others like taking risks and trying new things.

Respect others by supporting how *they* best meet the challenges of life. Living with someone who is always spouting orders and not giving latitude to who we are as an individual can be off putting. We may not even want to spend much time at home because of it. Having to meet someone else's expectations all the time is draining and despairing.

We cannot even dictate to ourselves how to grow or who to be, for eventually the truth of who we are will fight to find its way out of the false reality we have created, into the sun. If it does not, we simply wither in spirit, and most often die unfilled.

When we are opinionated and pushy with our loved ones, it is a sign that we are too invested in their lives, and need to pay more attention to our own. We think they should achieve either what we are trying to achieve, or what we want them to achieve, so *we* can feel better.

When we find ourselves interfering in other's lives and causing upset, we need only focus on and improve our own lives to set things right.

When we flourish in our own lives, not only do we cease to become a nuisance to others, but we also become a living example of self-actualization (coming into our own fruition). We teach by how we live rather than cramming our way down other people's throats. And if they continue to follow their own way, we might just be surprised that their way turns out better—for them.

This is respect. Respecting others will enrich all relationships.

Points to Remember

1. We all think and behave differently in accordance to who we are.

2. Choices that might crush us, might be what another uses as a springboard to do better.

3. Supporting others in choices that seem to work for them can greatly improve the quality of our relationships.

4. Rather than scorching children's self-esteem with hurtful words or a spanking, a more respectful alternative is to give them *natural* consequences in a loving manner.

5. Instead of encouraging our children to be socially admired, encourage them to be themselves and to do what is right, comfortable, and healthy for them as an individual.

6. Believing in people helps them shift their mental focus to the best of themselves.

7. When we try to micromanage the lives of others, we rob them of their journey toward fruition.

8. When we are opinionated and pushy with our loved ones, it is a sign that we are too invested in their lives, and need to pay more attention to our own.

9. When our interference in other people's lives causes upset, we need only focus on and improve our own lives to set things right.

18
WORK TOWARD FORGIVENESS

Everyone in the world has faltered. We all do what we do, and have all done what we have done at any given moment based on hundreds of factors not always visible for analyzing. We are complex beings, and we are *always* doing what we feel we must to survive. Forgiveness is understanding that. Life is hard and confusing for everyone at various times in our lives, and we are all doing the best we can, even if that best is not so good.

When we begin to forgive, we:

> *release toxic resentment that keeps us in the past
>
> *take greater pleasure in the now
>
> *realize that everyone is doing their best
>
> *can see that, in the long run, no one escapes consequences for their actions
>
> *learn from unsavory incidents to make our lives, or the lives of others better
>
> *have a deep appreciation for our own being

Forgiving Others

When we have been hurt, the normal human reaction is to be resentful. This means we are alive and are responding as we should—initially. However when resentment continues for years, or decades, it turns into a grudge that thwarts our well- being.

When we hold a grudge, we are cementing a *perception* of a person or event that we have decided is true. From our angle, we think we know enough to proclaim judgment. However, there are so many angles and dimensions to every person and act, beyond what we can know, and our opinion is just our opinion.

Depending on the severity of the offending incident or incidents, processing and healing times will vary. Our personalities and life experience also play a great factor.

When the grudge becomes toxic, our quality of life is compromised, and perhaps our relationships too.

How to Forgive Others

1. *Everyone is doing their best.* Realize that at the time of the offense, the offender was doing the best he or she could, given all the variables in their life. If the dots are traced back and connected to anyone beginning at birth, we would see how they came to be who they are, and perhaps why they did what they did.

If we could have access to the genetic composition of that person, we would further see the propensities he or she was born with, in combination with their life circumstance and experiences, that led them to be as they were at the time we felt assaulted.

2. *Accept that we are all different.* Sometimes our resentments stick because we can't imagine doing to another what was done to us. However, if we were that person with all the same variables, we might find ourselves in very different reality doing very different things. What we expect of ourselves, we tend to expect of others, whether it is possible for them or not.

3. *Release the notion that incidents are unfair.* Sometimes we find it hard to forgive because we feel we got the short end of the stick and the offenders are getting away with what they did. However, keep this in mind: *natural consequences are inevitable for all.* Life actually *is* fair. The chronic cheaters end up alone because eventually they gain a reputation not to be trusted. Those who give themselves away to help others, continually end up drained and empty. Those who chronically cast blame, carry an inner torment beyond imagination. Predators live in constant hell, that's why they keep trying to give it away to make others feel their reality.

This doesn't mean the offenders didn't violate us, or we them, but none could *at that time* help it, and we *can* turn any violation into a productive life experience.

This doesn't invalidate our pain or theirs, but it can shed a compassionate light on the internal suffering that leads anyone to ill-behavior.

This does not mean we have to take ill-behavior from anyone! We can always remove ourselves from offensive people, leaving them unable to abuse us any longer.

However, when we can see that our offenders are doing the best they can, it is easier to have compassion and hence . . . forgive. We all have different ways of coping, some healthy, some not. All we can do is find healthy ways for ourselves to handle what comes at us, and to control our output. Holding grudges only poisons our existence.

When we cling to the idea that we were done wrong, we perpetuate the pain. If we see our part in what happened, even if that part was being too trusting or giving too much, we can release the pain.

4. *Take excellent care of ourselves.* The path to forgiving others lies in taking excellent care of ourselves. When we nurture ourselves, we begin to heal from anything that has ever happened to us. We take steps that make us feel better. These steps, one by one, give us a feeling that we are taking charge of our lives.

5. *Learn from what happened.* As previously discussed in overcoming trauma, we can learn from what others have done to us, and use that learning as stepping stones toward a better life. A person who was raped may take self-defense and aid others enduring that trauma. A person who gambled all their money away, can start over by seriously addressing the addiction and finding new healthy ways to cope with stress. We can quite literally take any event that has ever happened to us, and transform it into something positive.

As tragic as some events might seem, there truly is a silver lining in every cloud if only we would lift our eyes to see.

Forgiving Ourselves

Guilt can weigh us down and greatly decrease our quality of living. Yet, going through the maze of life, we *all* will bump into walls and meet obstacles. We are not expected to come out of the womb and hit the ground running. Stumbling is not grounds to crucify anyone, including ourselves.

Everyone stubs their toes. It is part of the growing process. At one time or another, we do things we wished we didn't. We learn over time what works and what does not. In this, we have countless opportunities to improve our life situation. The act of self-thrashing only generates negative repercussions.

We all have regrets, some small, some big, because we are human, and deep down, all the same—weak and strong, frightened and brave, angry and loving. Even the darker more shadowed areas of ourselves play important parts in the makeup of who we are, who we attract into our lives, and the adventures yet before us.

We are who we are, born into the world with specific physical, emotional, and mental characteristics, and into a particular environment and situation. These are the cards we are dealt. It takes much time to learn how to survive with all the components of who we are as individuals, the environment we are in, and the situations we encounter. There are ups and downs to every trait, environment, and situation. There are gifts in every tragedy. There are challenges in every walk of life. No one can be all things, to all people, all the time. It is virtually impossible.

Therefore, it is to be expected that we will sometimes fail, sometimes be weak in certain areas, and sometimes get very confused and frightened in this big and demanding world.

> *"Experiencing life is noble.*
> *There are no failures or mistakes*
> *only innocent exploration with*
> *consequences that drive us*
> *to become more than we are."*

We all have short-comings and bad days. When we slip, that is normal, and accidents happen. It does not mean all is lost. When we are upset about wrong doing, consider how complicated life and living can be. It is difficult to see all, know all, and do all—just right, in the barrage of information and stimulation constantly coming at us. By doing it wrong, we learn how to get it right. If we choose to forgive ourselves, we can move on. We can rise from the ashes, transformed, and better than we were.

Points to Remember

1. We all do what we do, and have all done what we have done based on hundreds of factors not always visible for analyzing.

2. When we hold a grudge, we are cementing a *perception* of a person or event that we have decided is true.

3. Everyone is doing their best at any given time

4. Natural consequences for ill-behavior eventually catch up to everyone.

5. When we take excellent care of ourselves, we feel better and find it easier to forgive.

6. We can forgive ourselves more easily if we can learn from the regretful experience.

19
LOVE WITHOUT CONDITIONS

We often use the word love interchangeably with need. However, there is a difference. I need you is not I love you. *I need* means you are important to me because I need something from you. Love, in this context is conditional. *I love you if . . . (If I can't get it from you, I will either keep trying or find someone else to give it to me.)*

Unconditional love means we want others to behave in ways that are best for them, not *us*. To love another truly, a partner, a family member, our children, or our friends, we wish them the best, even if it means we don't get from them what we want or need.

Unconditional love *does not* mean we endure ill-treatment. We can love someone, but if ill-treated, can choose not to be around him or her.

Just as true love is about caring for others for *their* own sake, not ours, so it is that if others truly love us, it is for our sake, not theirs. Many parents carry this kind of love for their children, and humanitarians often carry this kind of love for the world.

When we love without conditions, we:

    *generate deep bonds with others

    *break unhealthy relationship patterns

    *pave the way for deep emotional intimacy

    *do not emotionally manipulate others to do our bidding

    *can respectfully detach from an abusive relationship

    *are less upset when verbally attacked

*have greater appreciation for ourselves

Romantic Love

A common precept of the romantic relationship is two halves
joining to make a whole. This perception often leads to conflict in
the relationship, as each becomes dependent on the other to get
their needs met. The couple then can become so bound that they
are not free to learn and grow as they may. It can be difficult to
flourish when our mates expect behaviors from us that serve
them, not us—and vice versa. The more incompatible the couple,
the more horrible the experience can be. The fear of being alone
to develop ourselves is often worse than our unfulfilling
relationship.

The more compatible the couple, the less this problem will arise.
However, the most successful unions are those with two
compatible people who support each other's personal growth,
despite the challenges it might present.

The Traps of Romance

1. *Projection.* We often project our idea of an ideal mate onto our
prospects, deciding that is who they are, even if they aren't. Or
we give the illusion that we are who our mates want us to be,
suppressing our true self. Eventually, the holographic projection
fades and the real person bleeds through, revealing the truth. In
this, the whole relationship will be reevaluated.

2. *Fear of rejection.* Fearing eventual rejection or abandonment,
we often are emotionally unavailable. We are in the relationship,
but we do not expose our true thoughts and feelings. We keep
our heart at a distance. True intimacy cannot be had and the
relationship can never deepen.

3. *Mistaking attraction for love.* Sexual attraction (chemistry) is
generally what we call being in love. We might be in love, even if
we are incompatible with the subject of our attraction. While
sexual attraction is nature's way of insuring propagation of the

species, it has nothing to do with an authentic connection between two people, or unconditional love. This is not to say there aren't couples who are in love and also love each other unconditionally.

However, if the couple in love is incompatible and/or even one of the two is not self-examined, unconditional love is difficult to achieve. Unresolved issues of either person, become obstacles for both. If the couple cannot see eye to eye, the romance dance becomes a series of missteps. It can work, if *both* members of the couple are willing to resolve their own issues and help the other solve theirs. If not, then conflict prevails.

Healing the Romantic Relationship

The true test of the relationship is for at least one member to have the courage to begin constructively meeting his or her own needs. Example: Your mate never wants to go anywhere with you. Instead of arguing about it, go off by yourself or with a friend, and have some fun, not as a ploy to punish your mate, but to genuinely enjoy yourself. Your mate will learn that you are not going to waste your time being upset, and that you don't need him or her to enjoy your day. Your partner will either love you more for this because the pressure is off; or missing you, step up to the plate and spend more time with you. The third possibility is that if your mate has a lot of undealt with emotional baggage, the relationship will be tested.

It takes two to have a healthy relationship steered by unconditional love. If one member can't face their issues, the relationship will perpetually suffer. However, personal growth, even in one member, will always break the stale pattern, and will one way or another create change in the relationship.

The more fulfilled we are within ourselves, the more we can unconditionally love our mate, even if that means a parting of the ways due to incompatibility. And the more we unconditionally love ourselves, the more we are enabled to end an unhealthy relationship.

Parental Love

We often expect our children to become what we think they should be, and raise them either the way we were, or the opposite, or to give us what *we* need. All of this is love *with conditions* and completely ignores the individuality of the child.

Children are whole people in developing bodies, new to the world, with unique traits and propensities. When we love them unconditionally, their thoughts and feelings always matter. We encourage their self-expression, teaching them healthy ways to emote. Example: If your angry child throws a toy, teach him to express anger with words, such as, "I'm mad!"

When we love our children unconditionally, we treat them as people first, and children second. We listen to their thoughts without judging them. We let them know we understand their point of view, and help them discover constructive ways to meet their challenges.

When we love our children unconditionally, we give them a wide berth to grow, while also providing a structured environment. Structure helps them feel safe, and fosters learning. Inappropriate behavior, met with natural consequences, rather than punishing (as earlier discussed), teaches them how to get along in life. A detailed example would be:

Your child won't come to the dinner table. Instead of yelling, threatening, or punishing, just eat dinner without your child. Clear the table. When your child eventually comes into the kitchen for food, say casually, even lovingly, "I called you for dinner but you didn't come. Dinner is over. Here are some healthy snacks (like vegetables, or not something very liked), to tide you over until breakfast. Your child might throw a tantrum, but will not likely miss coming to the table again for the next meal. It might take a time or two, but if done lovingly and consistently, the mission can be accomplished without assaulting their self-esteem.

With grown children, unconditional love means we let them lead their own lives. Insisting they adhere to our opinions is counterproductive; as they will likely do what they feel they must anyway.

When we share our opinions only if asked, the underlying message is, "I believe in you." When our children feel we believe in them, it empowers them to believe in themselves. Unconditional love used in this way is quite powerful. It also tightens the parent-child bond, generating great appreciation and love for each other.

If we fear for our children's safety, genuine concern can be shared, along with a confirmation of our belief in them to come through their challenges with flying colors. Example: "I am terribly worried about you dating that person, but I know you will take good care of yourself." Then we can step back, leave them to it, and focus on our own personal growth to feel better. Even drug interventions are done with loads of love, and not a punitive finger waggling. However, we can't force anyone to live constructively. Ultimately, everyone has to find their own way in life, bruised knees and all.

Familial Love

Unconditional love in the family is reflected by respecting each member. When family conflict arises, let each person be heard. Sometimes, with everyone's input, creative solutions may occur to satisfy all without anyone sacrificing too much. Let the focus be, "How can everyone win?" Not, "How can I win?" Ascertain whose needs seem greater at any given time to determine solutions. Consistently reevaluate the family's needs as time goes by. Each family member's voice is important, and if heard with respect, will continue to be a vital and pleasant addition to the family group.

Friendship

Unconditional love among friends is shown by being sensitive to each other's needs without compromising our own. It is having a balanced energy of give and take. No one is giving more or taking more, over all, even though at times, due to hardship one is doing more taking than giving.

Sometimes one friend is needier than the other and consistently does most of the taking. These are not the friendships that are treasured. If the needy one does not give back caring attention to the friend in equal measure *overall*, the unbalanced relationship will eventually end.

Unconditional Love for Ourselves.

Unconditional love is true love. It is the highest form of love we can have, and love's truest definition. When we love ourselves unconditionally, it is easy to love others the same. Knowing our worth is unconditional stimulates deep healing within ourselves. Thus, our output in life radiates confidence, honor, caring, and wisdom, enriching all facets of our lives.

Points to Remember

1. Unconditional love means we want others to behave in ways that are best for them, not *us*.

2. Unconditional love *does not* mean we endure ill-treatment.

3. Just as true love is about caring for others for *their* own sake, not ours, so it is that if others truly love us, it is for our sake, not theirs.

4. The most successful unions are those with two compatible people who support each other's personal growth, despite the challenges it might present.

5. The more fulfilled we are within ourselves, the more we can unconditionally love our mate, even if that means a parting of the ways due to incompatibility.

6. When we love our children unconditionally, we treat them as people first, and children second.

7. When we love our children unconditionally, we give them a wide berth to grow, while also providing a structured environment.

8. With grown children, unconditional love means we let them

lead their own lives, with the caveat of sharing our concern if need be.

9. When our children feel we believe in them, it empowers them to believe in themselves.

10. Unconditional love in the family is reflected by respecting each member.

11. Unconditional love among friends is shown by being sensitive to each other's needs without compromising our own, and overall having equal measure of give and take.

12. When we love ourselves unconditionally, it is easy to love others the same.

20
BE PRESENT

Life is made up of moments. Everything that ever happens to us, happens in a moment. This very moment is what feels most real. Painful past memories and fearing future calamity generally stress us more than *right now*.

When we live in the present, we:

*make the most of our lives here and now

*are less stuck in our bad memories

*are less frightened about the future

*can make a positive difference in our current life

*are open to opportunities right in front of us

*can appreciate what we do have

Fixating on the Past. *Don't get behind yourself.*

Our past is crowded with memories. These memories are colored by how we viewed events at that time in our life. A five-year-old seeing parents fight will be interpreted from a five-year-old point of view, not with the whole truth. Yet, the conclusions drawn at age five are alive in the present.

When we incessantly replay unsavory memories, we are living in the past. When we live in the past, we are lost in a collection of moments remembered by the *meaning we gave them then*, and not necessarily what actually was.

Fixating in a past of "what if and if only" and "would have, should have, and could have," keeps us there, cementing our reality in regrets, anger, and sorrow. In this, we keep alive our *version* of the truth. However, if we could see our past events from a bird's eye view, we would get a broader perspective of what really happened. We would see that everyone involved was struggling and doing the best they could with the cards they were dealt. If we were to go back in time *without* hindsight and a perfect storm of conditions identical, we all would do exactly the same thing.

Given this, the past is the past. Let it go. Let it go. Let it go. Letting the past go is easier if we make a resolution to learn from it. What lessons can we learn? And how can we use those lessons to change our present. For example, if we were scarred by how our parents raised us, we can raise our children differently. If we were mean to someone and regret it, we can treat others even better than we would have without that past action, from this moment on.

Use lessons of the past to change the present.

Fixating on the Future. *Don't get ahead of yourself.*

When we live in the future, our every move is about what might happen tomorrow. Yet, what we think might happen in the future is generated by our state of mind today. Our state of mind is altered every time an event occurs, even if only a little. Therefore, by the time we get to our projected future, we have changed from who we were when we imagined it.

Our future is further influenced by the wild cards we are thrown along the way, life's little surprises, the unexpected events, some welcomed, some not.

So, perseverating about the future is mostly a barren pursuit. Whatever we imagine our future will be, it won't be. It might be close but not the same, and more likely so different it never crossed our minds.

While we must to some extent take precautions and save for a rainy day, throwing ourselves into the future makes us lose out on today. Enjoyable new memories are not made today because our mind is always on tomorrow.

The peace we seek in wanting a secure future can be found within ourselves, right now. If our security is within, and we believe in ourselves to handle anything, we can breathe easier about whatever the future presents. Worrying less about an unsavory future, we can better enjoy the pleasantries of the moment.

Living in the Now

When we live in the now, we appreciate the moment and make the most of every day. Tomorrow may never come, and yesterday is gone. When we live in the moment, we can find peace in everything we do. When we brush our teeth, we appreciate that we have a toothbrush and paste to clean them, and the ability to chew our food. We appreciate we have hands to brush our teeth.

How wonderful that we have a body, and eyes to see, ears to hear, that we can taste, smell, and touch.

How wonderful that we have at least one person in our life that seems to care about us, or an animal that brings us comfort, or a child to love.

How wonderful that we can always find stars in the sky, and oceans to behold, mountains to climb, and trees to enjoy.

Today is today.

One step at a time, and live each step to the fullest. Driving to work, enjoy music on the radio, or silence if you need that. Enjoy the scenery and tell yourself you are embarking on a brand new day of adventure. What will happen today in the story of your life?

Going about your morning routine, live it as if it might be the last time you do it and find joy along the way in the little things. The flowers in your garden, the breeze upon your face, the smile of a child, the wagging tail of a dog.

Going to bed, enjoy the bedding and the bedroom, and the sweet night when you have the opportunity to recuperate and have some night adventures in your dreams.

If in turmoil, then focus only on what you can do right now, today, to make your life better. One . . . step . . . at . . . a . . . time.

In short, appreciate what you have. Be open to the growth and change ever knocking on your door, if only you can be here now to hear it.

Living in an enriched present is all in the attitude. When we open our minds to enjoy our day, and believe in ourselves to meet our challenges, so much of our fear subsides, freeing us to live a fuller life.

Only here and now can we create change that will make a painful past not so bad, and a better chance of a greater future.

Points to Remember

1. Looping on old painful memories perpetuates anguish.

2. When living in the past, we relive events remembered by the *meaning we gave them then*, and not necessarily what actually was.

3. Predicating our current happiness on what must happen in the future is stressful.

4. The peace we want in the future can be found right now. within ourselves.

5. The present is the point of power.

6. The moment is really the only reality that matters.

7. What you do this moment will dictate your reality.

8. When we live in the now, our life is more enriched.

21
GROW NATURALLY

The seasons come and go, naturally. Weather has its cycles. Our bodies too. We develop in the womb, are born, we age, we die. An apple seedling becomes a sprig, the sprig a tree, and eventually the tree bears apples.

When we try to force our goals, it is like trying to make the apples grow before they go through the growing process. Working toward goals is one thing, insisting they happen right now fosters stress, worry, and perhaps disappointment born from forcing issues.

When we let ourselves grow naturally, we:

*are less stressed and therefore kinder to those around us

*honor our own unfolding into who we truly are

*don't push our goals to happen, but rather nurture them along

*don't decide *how* we should be growing, but celebrate whatever way we can grow

*go with our *own* flow

Discover your purpose.

When working toward anything we generally see the end game. We see our bedroom clean before we begin to clean it, and holding that idea in place helps us achieve the task. We see a project done before we begin to work on it, and keep that vision in place until the project is accomplished. However, seeing an end game such as marrying a perfect mate, or winning the lottery, is often met with disappointment as we are bypassing a highly significant matter. Everything born has a genetic predisposition. Just as everything grows into what it is, so do we.

However, what we are designed to be is often a mystery until we actually get there. For instance, throwing all our energy into attracting the perfect mate is like betting on a pipe dream. Who we are deep down emits an energy, and that energy attracts or repels others as well as life events. We are who we are, and we attract who we attract.

We might think we know what we want in a mate, but in the end, who we are, our energy, our personality will attract what it will. A dominating person will likely be attracted to one who subjugates. A needy person will generally seek a strong savior type of mate. However, this is as it should be. The challenges that arise due to these attractions give opportunity for serious growth.

We might decide that we are going to be rich and can make that happen if we just see the end game, using all our mind power. While mind power is a real thing, again, who we are deep down, the energy we are made of, our personality and constellation in life will ensure that we grow the way we need to grow, and will attract to us what we need, beyond what we think we need. Example: If we attract negative money issues, it doesn't mean we are bad. It means the way we are put together is presenting challenges that force us to grow.

Financial challenges are often had by overly generous people who tend to be selfless and spend money on others, or overly selfish people who lavish in what they want, or chronic victims that set themselves up to be in peril.

Those who are sitting well financially (other than celebrities) often are more logical, less emotional types, or very driven and practical, or thieves.

How much money one has is not always in proportion to what they make. It is who we are that decides that. So trying to make the perfect mate come along, or deciding we will win a pile of money is not taking into account that we are who we are, and we, like the apple tree will grow into who we are meant to be.

Just like various flowers might attract more bees than others because of their biochemistry, location, etc., we are no different.

Once we accept our natures, we begin to grow naturally, and in directions that are true to ourselves. We take what comes and we take it in stride. While we might work hard or take a break, if we keep in mind that the better 'no lose end game' is to grow into who we are and to be all we can be. Let the end game be self-actualization, whatever that is.

Thinking like this melts away stress and fosters self-belief. All you need do *is be true to yourself.* We each have unique gifts, sometimes realized, sometimes not. But in growing naturally into our true self, we discover the beauty within us and set if free into the world. By growing into who we are, we discover our true purpose for living.

Points to Remember

1. Forcing our goals to be achieved fosters stress, worry, and often disappointment.

2. Growing naturally is to honor the way we are put together which presents challenges that give opportunity for serious growth.

3. Growing naturally into who we are takes us in a life direction that resonates with our true selves.

4. When we grow into who we are, we discover our inner beauty and share it with the world.

22
LIGHTEN UP

Lighten up.

Most of us experience far more anxiety than necessary. We have this whole inner world we decide is true and live in it, such as, *I am ashamed about my debt. I don't deserve anything good to happen to me.*

When we are caught in the quagmire of our worry, we are often blind to what is going on around us. If we would but stop the spinning of that story for a moment and poke our head outside our turbulent inner world, we might see something altogether different.

Is the cat looking up at us wanting affection? Is there a rainbow outside our window? Sometimes when we stop and look around us, we calm down, realizing our tense world is not THE world, but *a perception* we are having about what is happening to us, what has happened to us, or what might happen to us.

When we lighten up, we:

   *realize things are not as dire as we make them

   *get perspective, and are less hard on ourselves

   *loosen up on what we must do, and the way we must do it

   *are calmer regarding other people's mistakes

   *live a more enjoyable existence

Stop feeding the drama.

When we stop and pay attention to the world around us, it can calm the turbulent world within us. The beautiful rose, the purring cat, the smile of a child, the touch of love, a cup of tea or coffee. Really, is what we perceive to be tragic, so tragic, or just our perception of the moment?

Things are only as drastic as we make them, and this includes tragic incidences. Far away from the drama, the sun is shining, the stars are out, and rainbows are springing everywhere. Roses still smell good, morning coffee or tea is still wonderful. Our worth is intrinsic, so never at risk. The ones who *really* love us, still love us. We can still enjoy a good movie, book, game, sport, music, nature, or artistic expression.

> *Take a time out from stress*
> *and enjoy the little things.*

Even in the darkest times, we can take time to enjoy our day. A little bit of fun goes a long way to helping us recover from stress.

General Techniques for Lightening Up

1. *View your life as a comedy.* Many comedians do an excellent job of helping us see the funny side of horrible. They take the serious and give us a lighter perspective.

We too can do that with our own lives. In a comedy, we laugh at stressful situations because we can relate, and we don't feel so alone.

Example: If the star of the comedy is running late for an important meeting, and can't find her dress shoes, so she has to wear sneakers. Tick tock. She can't find her car keys, the cat goes into labor, and the toilet is overflowing. Tick tock. We watch her cursing, and upset, yet as a viewer, it is quite funny.

Viewing our own lives through the eyes of comedy can help us lighten up and laugh at ourselves.

Imagine you are on the movie screen, and you are being watched by others who take an interest because they can relate. Hence, you actually make them feel better about themselves for similar experiences they have had, or will have.

We often associate failure or a why me attitude to these stressful events, but really, it is just life, and everything that has happened to you has happened to hundreds and thousands and millions of others at some point in their lives. Our personalities are different, our motives will vary, our coping skills can be constructive to tragic, but deep down, *we are all the same.*

2. *Have Fun.* Pursue what you enjoy even if you feel there is no time or money, and/or you are depressed. This will boost your energy and give you a reason to wake up in the morning. If we don't treat ourselves to enjoyment despite our circumstance, anxiety and depression can more easily get a foothold. Have some fun, even if it is quick and simple, such as playing the guitar for five minutes, or watching that comedy.

We often feel we can't have fun until this or that is done. However, it is critical that we have a soft period of time away from our worries and responsibilities. Take time out to play with your kid, fetch with your dog, or even a video game with a friend. Or, just take a bit of time to enjoy a favorite simple pleasure.

Having fun can renew our energy to do our tasks more efficiently.

3. *Do meaningful things.* Everyday do something meaningful, such as having a good conversation, or writing that long overdue letter to your friend, or taking time to pet the cat.

4. *Focus on the good things.* Just like a television station, we can change the channel from thoughts that upset us to thoughts that make us feel better. When overwhelmed, change your mental channel to what brightens your spirits, such as reminiscing about all the good things you have done, or regarding the people who love you.

When overwhelmed with bad feelings,
change your mental channel.

LIGHTEN UP!

Points to Remember

1. When we stop and look around us at the nicer things of life, we calm down, realizing our tense world is not THE world, but *a perception* we are having about what is happening to us, what has happened to us, or what might happen to us.

2. Things are only as drastic as we make them.

3. View your life as a comedy, and learn to laugh at yourself.

4. Deep down, we are all the same, experiencing what millions of others endure.

5. Pursue what you enjoy even if you feel there is no time or money, and or you are depressed.

6. Everyday, do something meaningful.

7. Focus on the good things.

8. Lighten up.

23
FOLLOW YOUR DREAMS

We hear it often, "Follow your dreams," but it is not always that simple. There are snags along the way, and sometimes the dream we are following changes. And sometimes, we can't even find a dream to pursue at all. However, when we can find something that makes us want to get out of bed in the morning, and nourishes us deep down, it is a dream worth fighting for with everything inside us.

When we find and follow our dreams, we:

*feel invigorated and excited to live

*feel a sense of purpose and a strong life direction

*feel peace within ourselves

The Stale Gray Life

Sometimes we know what our dreams are, and sometimes we don't. It is wonderful to have a passionate drive to manifest a dream, but not everyone can feel that. Many are just bored in life and can't seem to find an interest that makes them want to get out of bed in the morning.

When bored, we usually have little in our life that stimulates us, even if we are very busy. This is compounded by looking too much out at the world and too little inside ourselves. And the search continues to find something that floats our boat.

Keeping our spirits up can prove challenging when we cannot find an interest that lights that spark of excitement, and maybe even give us a joyful life direction. When we try too hard to find it, we are generally met with frustration and disappointment.

 The best way to find something that impassions us is to first spend more time alone with ourselves. Our outer world can pull us into currents of activity that drown out what is deep inside us. To get in touch, we need alone time to quiet and clear the murky waters.

Technique for Finding a Dream

Find a quiet place to be alone, perhaps lying in your yard looking up at the clouds, or at night, the stars, or even in your bed when there is no one else around. Relax into yourself. When your mind goes outward thinking of tasks, duties, and other people, redirect it inward to become aware of what you wish could be, if only wishes came true.

Daydream. Imagine what would bring joy and brightness to you even if it seems illogical, or impossible, or a waste of time. Give it at *least* five minutes. If it is difficult at first, give yourself many opportunities to grease wheels and get your imagination going. This will give you clues to who you are and what you need, to be more fulfilled in life. It will also give you clues to what isn't right in your life, or what is holding you back.

For instance, you might daydream about a kind person who gives you a lot of attention. This is likely telling you that you don't have that in your life right now. So the next course of action to finding a dream to follow, might be to address the primary people in your life, how you are treated, and take steps to better that situation.

Once that obstacle is cleared, you are one layer closer to beholding the next step to finding your dream. The next time you let your mind imagine, it might, for example, be that you are a famous scientist. This is telling you that science is an interest that uplifts you. In this, you might start spending more time in science museums or pursue science in school, or even read more about your area of interest, maybe even start doing experiments.

By continuing to follow what lights you, step by step, you move toward a dream that perhaps you didn't even know you had.

The more you take time to look in the quiet still waters of yourself, the more you will discover who you are, what motivates you, what doesn't, what you enjoy and what you don't. Follow what makes you feel better, and see where it leads you.

Dream Chasing

Sometimes we have the dream that we are chasing . . . and chasing . . . and chasing. We are tired of chasing it, but we are told to follow our dreams and never give up. While following our dreams gives us something to live for, if we throw everything we have into it and the doors aren't opening, and our knuckles are bruised from knocking, and our feet are getting injured from walking . . . STOP.

This doesn't mean we are giving up on our dreams, or, maybe we are, but one thing is for certain: When we pursue our goals forcefully, pushing on to the death, we invite destruction.

We all know what happens when the levees break, or when winds gather momentum destroying things. When we *force* our objective, it often backfires, perhaps on our health, or in our relationships. We might even inadvertently sabotage the very dream we are pursuing.

Persistence is a wonderful thing. However, if our prolonged effort to achieve a goal is not yielding desired results, be open to try another way. When persistence turns to stubbornness, despite outcome, we hurt ourselves.

Working steadfastly with fortitude toward a dream is healthy when tempered with patience. There is a natural time table for everything in life. When we move naturally toward our dream, driven by inner strength, and born from joy and excitement to "do this thing", we can still enjoy our present and foster growth in other areas of our life.

When we move with the time table that is naturally upon us, we do not metaphorically rip the caterpillar out of its cocoon prematurely. In this, allowing the caterpillar to transform into the butterfly, our goals can be realized without collateral damage.

Don't push, flow.

When we see ourselves akin to a mighty river forging a natural path to the sea, we will come into our dreams naturally. Wherever we focus, there we will go.

When feeling depleted or frustrated in pursuing goals, stop, rest, and regroup. Take a short vacation from the endeavor. Desperation usually works against us. People can smell it, and often recoil. These are the doors slamming in your face. Anything we *force* will be met with push back.

Confidence, however, is *very* attractive.

In relaxing and letting the dream go for a while, we are able to open up and let the sun shine in. In this light, we might realize a different dream that perhaps is at our fingertips, but we couldn't see it because we had tunnel vision for the old dream.

Or we might have light shed on a whole new way of going about pursuing our dream.

Yes, by all means, follow your dreams, tempered with flexibility on how and when you get there.

Dreams are not always big.

Sometimes it is the smaller dreams that give the most satisfaction. These dreams are present in our deep down yearnings, such as the need for alone time, to be creative, to repair a relationship, get healthy, have time to enjoy the simple things of life, or to do something meaningful. These seemingly smaller dreams, when pursued in a healthy manner, nurture and heal us deep within. We are taking steps that are in keeping with who are and what we need as a unique human being.

Actualizing these simpler dreams results in pure, heartfelt acts that make us shine. We can live a quite satisfying life by actualizing smaller dreams such as: expressing ourselves through art, craft, cooking, writing, music, dance, acting, or communicating productively; getting on an exercise regime, and eating nourishing foods; learning to have fun; communing with nature; having meaningful conversations, or making new friends; caring more for animals, or joyfully tending a garden; decorating our home or body; joining a club of interest; or volunteering somewhere.

Pursue your own dream.

It is important that the dream you pursue is not a dream someone else has for you. For instance, your parents want you to be a lawyer, so you pursue law school, even though your heart lies in horticulture. Pursuing any old dream will not yield joy in living. The dream must be your dream. A dream you have for yourself.

Pursue your own dream.

This also means that we do not expect others to be responsible for our dream to come true. If our dream is for our child to be a doctor, or our mate to make a lot of money, we need to find another dream. The dream we follow must stimulate our own unfolding and awakening into something more, if it is to take us to a rewarding finish line.

And if others stand in our way, it is for us to gently forge ahead while still respecting those around us.

The fruit of our efforts are felt most when we *evolve ourselves rather than trying to get others to uplift us.* In this, we are loyal to our quintessential being, and to our own life story. No one can do our growing for us.

Following our dreams is finding ourselves.

When we find a dream to follow that lights us up inside we are finding ourselves. In this big and crazy world, this can so often be confusing and hard to achieve. However, actualizing dreams, big or small, one or many, that better our lives, brings us closer to actualizing our potential. Then, at our life's end, there are no regrets, not even for setbacks because we know we were brave. We weathered the storm and drove ourselves onward toward our own transformation as a human being from ordinary to extraordinary.

Points to Remember

1. The best way to find something that impassions us is to first spend more time alone with ourselves.

2. Daydreams can give us clues to dreams we can actualize.

3. Follow what makes you feel productively better, and see where it leads you.

4. If hitting roadblocks to achieving our dreams, be open to try another way, or another dream.

5. When we move naturally toward our dream, we can still enjoy our present and foster growth in other areas of our life.

6. Don't push, flow.

7. Dreams are not always big.

8. Follow a dream that is yours, not what you dream for another, or what another dreams for you.

9. Following a dream is finding ourselves.

24
EMBRACE CHANGE

Everything is always changing. We can't stop it. Without change, nothing can grow. Resisting change stems from fearing the unknown. Feeling safe is critical for most of us. Sometimes we cling to the familiar, even if we don't particularly like it. A stable present is often preferred to a mysterious future.

We are human, frailties and all, in the dark much of the time, unsure of so many things. As we grow older, our experiences give us wisdom, and we have an opportunity to become *enlightened*. The most enlightened are often the same people who were once among the most lost and confused in a shadowed past. It is never too late to shake off the dust and grow into our potential. Never.

When we embrace change, we:

    *invite personal development

    *realize change presents potential growth into something better

    *realize that embracing change is synonymous with believing in ourselves

    *relieve the stress that comes from resisting it

Letting Go

Letting go can be painful if we have to give up a situation we like, such as being released from an enjoyable job or saying goodbye to someone we love. Instead of looking at what we are losing, if we look forth to new possibilities, we can feel better. So, by accepting the changing situation, we open ourselves to the next chapter in our lives to see where it takes us.

Sometimes change can be frightening, even though we are not particularly happy with our current situation. However, our growth depends on change, despite how insecure we may feel when change is on the horizon. Change is met more smoothly when our security is rooted in ourselves.

The greatest surety of all is knowing we can count on ourselves to survive and thrive, no matter what the future holds. Having a resolute belief in ourselves serves us like a turtle with its shell, ever having a home no matter where it goes. Our safe haven can never be taken away.

When seeking life change, we must constructively tweak the way we think, the way we feel about ourselves, and the way we communicate. When we take it upon ourselves to nurture our being in ways we wish others would, we begin to view a change in who we thought we were and see who we are becoming. The outside world then, becomes a reflection of our inside world.

Change what goes on within you,
and you will change what goes on around you.

Change can feel wonderful if we go with the flow, roll with the punches, and keep looking to the beauty of life. Going with the flow is easier than resisting it. If the changes we seek seem to take too long, focus on fostering personal growth, and eventually the outside world will match it.

If change incites fear, know that it is time to grow. Our own evolution has come knocking on the door. We are just as much a part of the ever-changing natural world as anything else in it.

Points to Remember

1. Everything is always changing, including us.

2. Change is growth.

3. Embracing change is easier when our security comes from

within.

4. Going with the flow is easier than resisting it.

5. When seeking life change, we must constructively tweak the way we think, the way we feel about ourselves, and the way we communicate.

6. Change what goes on within you, and you will change what goes on around you.

25
BE GENUINE

Being a chameleon in uncomfortable situations often feels more secure than letting our true self shine through. If we are genuine, *they* might *get* us, or at the least, not like us.

When we feel this way, it is wise to remember that the diversity of weaknesses and strengths has allowed humans to survive as a collective. In addition, as different as we can be, we are also, as previously discussed, at our core, all the same: striving, fearing, loving, hating, hoping, and hurting.

Disclosure of our authentic selves connects us to our core sameness, which generates positive bonding. When someone proclaims something that we too have experienced, but kept a secret, we feel so much better that we are not the only one. We also feel much closer to that person. Or, perhaps that disclosure is to better a condition, such as standing up to something unethical, then others, secretly feeling the same way, are encouraged to speak up too. This also promotes positive bonding between people.

When we are genuine, we are always reminding ourselves who we really are, frailties and all. Given how easy it is to get swept up into other peoples realities, authenticity can anchor us to our true self. We need never be ashamed of our weaknesses, but rather accept them as challenges to grow stronger.

When we are genuine, we:

   *do not live behind a mask to hide our true self

   *need no affirmation, though affirmation is nice

   *do not need to control others, or what goes on around us because we have control of ourselves and what goes on within us *cannot be hurt, or at least for long, because we know who we are, and are ever open to learn and grow

Being genuine does not mean we constantly spout our truth.

We can remain authentic and not expose ourselves everywhere we go. Spouting what we think and feel all the time is not always appropriate. Speak when compelled and within the scope of your well-being. For instance, when in a group with a certain belief system, it may not be the time to proclaim we feel the opposite. We can still remain true to ourselves and move on.

It does, however, mean that if something goes against our grain, we honor ourselves enough to speak up.

Authenticity versus Game Playing

Authenticity is more powerful than playing psychological games. Instead of trying to incite reactions from others, when we are direct and honest we cut to the chase and get results quicker. For instance, if we are upset that our mate forgot our birthday, forget the silent treatment, hurling accusations, or trying to induce guilt. Just say what is bothering you. "It seems you forgot my birthday. I feel hurt."

If we have overreacted by being mean to someone due to past hurts, instead of keeping our pride and letting the situation ride, we can just say, "I had a rough past regarding . . . and I took it out on you. I am so sorry."

Genuineness invokes trust and respect, and makes us more beloved and easier to live with. At our core, the reasons we do anything sprouts from valid roots. Expressing honestly instead of protectively masking our true selves, not only helps others understand who we are really are, but we also can better understand and appreciate ourselves.

When we are genuine, we allow ourselves to develop and take shape to find our place in the world.

We are each a jewel.
Clean off the dirt, and shine!

Points to Remember

1. Disclosure of our authentic selves connects us to the core sameness of others, which generates positive bonding.

2. Being genuine anchors us to our true self.

3. We can remain authentic and not expose ourselves everywhere we go.

4. Authenticity is more powerful than playing psychological games.

5. Genuineness invokes trust and respect, making us more beloved and easier to live with.

26
LOOK TO THE BEAUTY

We humans often focus on what ails us. Sometimes this is helpful, and sometimes it leads to drawing closed-minded conclusions about why our problem exists and what that means for us. For instance, *I am failing in school. This means I am stupid and have no future.*

Whether our reality is based on actual truth or not, we experience it as if it *were* true, hence it is true for us. Our solutions then are often predicated on flawed assumptions. *I am stupid so I am just going to drop out.* Getting a tutor or changing classes isn't an option.

We can become obsessed with our conclusions, cementing them so strongly, we forget the stars are in the sky, or that simple kindness can rock the world.

We can't appreciate the gentle touch of a loved one, or the food we have in our refrigerator and what it took to get it there. The beauty of life is obscured by the gloomy picture we have painted in our heads.

There will always be something in our life we seek to improve, and another bump in the road, so premising our happiness on a smooth ride through life *ensures* a stressful existence. Life is made up of opposites. Up and down, in and out, light and dark, positive and negative, and so on. Life is what it is. Where we put our focus will determine how we experience it.

When we look to the beauty, we:

  *do not get lost in negatives

  *can find peace, even in the midst of chaos

  *can see the good that comes from hardship

*are appreciative of what we have, and what is working

Beauty is always there.

It is possible to navigate through unsettling experiences and still be inspired by the beautiful things of life. While walking along, lost in the emotion fueled by our struggle, the little flower can bring much joy if only we peek through the window of our world to see it.

Instead of shooing our loved one away when grumpy because we aren't in the mood to interact, look upon the kindly face and behold the great gift of that person. Maybe they aren't there to annoy us. Maybe, they have a kindly intention and we just can't see it because we are too steeped in our self-created distress. Maybe just maybe, if we behold what is knocking on our door or what is all around us, we can be lifted into a better mood.

How often have we sent people packing because we assume their intention is unkind? How often have we been sent packing, misunderstood by the significant people in our lives? This intolerance, no matter who it comes from, begets more suffering for all involved. We can get so steeped in our suffering that we can no longer discern the metaphorical medicine at hand.

While our problems must be addressed, a simple tweaking in how we cope with what ails us can go a long way toward bringing us the joy we seek, right now, *no matter what is going on.*

Nothing in our life needs to change to feel joy now. In fact, there is a great power in beholding joy. Our interpretation of the quagmire we are in suddenly shrinks and becomes a non-issue in the backdrop of incredible beauty.

When we change the channel of despair, to one of appreciation, we change our reality. The reality we experience is not a reaction to what is out there, but a reaction to how we *perceive* what is out there and the subsequent conclusions drawn. Look to the beauty to find balance and joy in life . . . right now. We are getting older every day and many of us are missing the beauty all around us and not celebrating what we have. However, if it should suddenly be taken from us, then we come to feel the remorse of not truly appreciating what we had.

Appreciate what you have now.

We are all explorers in this world, navigating our way through a deluge of emotional, mental, and physical territory in a constant quest to feel better. There are pitfalls and victories, ups and downs. This is to be expected. Pitfalls do not mean we have failed, but rather are a reflection of our bravery. Emerging from the womb, we embark on a great adventure. We are forced to be brave, endure hardship, stumble upon unexpected beauty, and shoot for the moon. Along the way we make discoveries that continually change our reality.

In time, we stop repeating worn out patterns and write a healthy script for ourselves. The beauty of it all is that we are *not* helpless. Our well-being is predicated on our state of mind. We may not be able to control what goes on around us, but as previously discussed, we can control what goes on *inside* us.

Attitude is everything. Everything always exists, good, bad, dark, light, tragedy, triumph. In that, we can choose to process our reality by looking at the silver lining in everything.

Beauty is born from tragedy every day. A typhoon strikes down thousands and the multitudes open their hearts and rally with an outpouring of aid. A loved one is killed violently and family members fight to change laws. Villains set the stage for heroes. Germs can strengthen our immune system. Every challenge is an opportunity for positive growth.

Look to the beauty, and even when working on a problem, keep your eyeballs there!

Points to Remember

1. Premising our happiness on a smooth ride through life, *ensures* a stressful existence.

2. It is possible to navigate through unsettling experiences and still be inspired by the beautiful things of life.

3. Nothing in our life needs to change to feel joy now.

4. When we change the channel of despair, to one of appreciation, we change our reality.

5. Our well-being is predicated on our state of mind.

6. Attitude is everything.

7. Beauty is born from tragedy everyday.

8. Look to the beauty, and even when working on a problem, keep your eyeballs there!

27
STAY CENTERED

When we are centered, we feel in balance. We walk the tightrope with ease as we cross the hills and valleys of our lives. Centeredness is ultimately a state of mind, and can be experienced even in chaos.

When centered, we do not judge, condemn, or fear. Our center is a place *within* us where all worries are released, and a calm healing power resides. This state of mind can quite literally change the course of our lives, as our responses to everything are wiser.

When we are centered, we:

 *take control of our lives, instead of being controlled by our lives

 *are less likely to be reactive in ways that work against us

 *feel more relaxed no matter what is going on around us

 *develop an inner power that can withstand anything

Meditation

The best way to get centered is to meditate. The word meditation often evokes an image of mysticism. However, meditation is simply the act of doing two things at once: relaxing and focusing. We do this all the time without realizing. We must relax and focus to achieve any endeavor. When the focus is on finding our center, that too can be achieved. In meditation, we learn to quiet the chatter in our heads and listen, really listen to what lies beneath the mundane level of our lives. Meditating can help us feel calm, in alignment (opposite of out of sorts) emotionally bright, and clear-minded.

There are many meditation methods. Here is an easy one:

1. Find a quiet spot, preferably in nature, or at least imagine yourself in the natural world, wherever you feel most soothed.

2. Set your intent toward internal balance, and self-actualization (becoming all you can be)

3. Quiet your mind. Soothing or stirring instrumental music can be played if that is helpful.

4. Focus on your breathing: slow, deep, and steady.

5. Let go of the outside world and ignore the chattering in your head that can keep you there.

6. As you grow calmer, turn your focus inward. See a tunnel of light that leads to your core being, akin to the center of a circle. See yourself there. When you arrive, you are centered.

7. At this point, you have stopped thinking. You have stopped looking outward to make sense of things. You are now listening, and looking into the clear still pond of your inner being.

8. Continue your breathing: slow, deep, and steady, focusing only on staring into the clear water. Do not direct your thoughts. Just watch and listen and see what happens. When in your center, deep down, you know what is right for you, and that part of you will show you what you need to see. Images will form. You can see what we could not see before. You gain insight, and clarity about your life, and life itself.

The more we practice this, the more we will be able to see an overview of how our life events got us to where we are, what we have learned along the way, and even where we are going. We can get a sense of our life purpose, see the good that came from our hardship, and have compassion for our struggles. In this centered mind state, we can experience the joy we have been trying to attain all along.

Although this takes practice, doing it everyday, even for a few minutes, will deepen the experience. Once we get used to being centered, we can bring that mind state into our everyday living.

We can recall this centered feeling instantly at any given time by creating a personal motto, such as, "I love myself," and/or seeing an image, such as yourself sitting peacefully by a waterfall. With our centered self at the helm, driving our lives, our reality changes for the better.

When centered, we can
regain or maintain an inner calm.

Sometimes we lose control of ourselves.

As we are human, there will be times when we lose control of ourselves. While this isn't generally a peachy experience, it can have merit. These unexpected emotional outbursts can be cathartic, expose underlying psychological wounds that need our attention, give others a chance to aid us, and be an example for others that it isn't the end of the world if it happens.

It is imperative to remember that all the guidelines in this book are just guidelines in general. Our deeper selves will always rise when necessary and do the unexpected in a therapeutic attempt to survive. However, by practicing these guidelines, we are nourishing our deep down selves, which is incredibly soothing, and more importantly, empowering. In this, not only is the likelihood of losing self-control minimized, but if we do lose it, we know how to get it back.

Although it is natural to feel derailed when we get in a car accident, contract a disease, lose a job or a loved one, or are singled out or trounced upon, it is only our *perception* of the occurrence, and not the occurrence itself that is causing the distress. The perception of, *this is a bad thing*, perpetuates the fear that we are losing some control over our lives. When this happens, a brief meditation can quickly set us right. This can be done anywhere at anytime by relaxing and focusing on our center.

We can only be shaken by the outer world if we allow those events to shake our inner world. *We can always maintain control of our lives, if we keep control of ourselves.* Sitting in the eye of the storm, out of the fray, can be quite empowering.

*We find peace in the outer world by
by finding peace in the inner world*

The Law of Attraction

The true law of attraction is less about keeping our mind focused on what we want to happen, then actually changing our state of being. When we are centered, we attract completely different experiences than when we feel out of sorts. We process events in ways that enrich our lives rather than feeding toxic drama. In this centered mind state, we can feel completely satisfied, in the very moment we are in.

Points to Remember

1. Centeredness is ultimately a state of mind, and can be experienced even in chaos.

2. Our center is a place *within* us where all worries are released, and a calm healing power resides.

3. The best way to get centered is to meditate.

4. Our perception of undesired occurrences can make us feel worse than the actual events, if we view them as losing some control over our lives.

5. Brief meditations, which are relaxation and focus, can quickly center us when our perceptions steer us in undesirable directions.

6. When centered, we attract different experiences than when we feel out of sorts.

28
LIVE THE MYSTERY

Suffice it to say, many incredible things occur that defy explanation and even logic. There is much we do not know or understand, but what is . . . still is.

Even in science, scientifically held truths are often altered when a new discovery is made. How many more discoveries will be made over the next thousands of years that will alter our currently held facts?

Beyond our beliefs and beyond what we feel we have proven true is yet the mystery.

We can, if we choose, put less energy into trying to demystify life with beliefs, logic, or seemingly proven facts, and actually live the mystery. We can welcome what we do not know. Welcome the wild card, and the things of which we cannot make sense.

When we live the mystery, we:

    *live life as an adventure

    *seize the day

    *accelerate personal growth

    *make the most out of our lives

    *are open to amazing occurrences

    *have a greater appreciation for life.

Define less, and experience more.

More opportunity would come our way if we would but have a *less defining attitude about life, such as I wonder what will happen today, not I know what will happen today, or I am afraid of what might happen today.* We can, if we choose, meet our days and moments with a strong heart, eager for adventure. When our attitude is soured, we close doors. We do not respond to those wants from deep down inside us. We fear taking the steps necessary to have it. In this, we are choosing to live a quiet but stable life, albeit somewhat unfulfilled. Everyone has a right to make this choice.

If, however, this uneventful and perhaps mildly depressing existence becomes an intolerable rut, there is a way out. Stop thinking about why things need to stay the same, and move in directions that ignite your motivation to get out of bed in the morning. These are the calls of the heart.

Yet, when our hearts call, we so often stuff our ears with logic. We deny that tiny voice that tells us there can be more for us in life, because it seems improbable or unfeasible.

But we can, at any point, take that leap of faith into who we are beyond what we can understand, and discover profound capabilities we didn't know we had. Blind trust in anything can prove regretful. However, blind trust in ourselves is as opening a door to our unrealized potential.

Answering our heart calls might begin with something as simple as watching the sun rise, or as complex as freeing ourselves from an addiction. We may not even understand what our heart is calling for at all, but just that it is calling. For instance, you want to be alone all day and do nothing, but it doesn't make any sense, or it is too hard to make happen. Find a way to do it, and see where it takes you.

Opening to the purity of your essence without trying to make sense of it, gives rise for great things to happen. You are not betting on your dream. You are betting on yourself to grow into your full potential without defining what that is. For example, "My potential lies in being a great artist, mother, and wife." Instead say, "I am open to discover and nurture all my potentials, whatever they may be."

Discover yourself!

Not knowing, or at least, not fully knowing the complexities of our total being, or even life in an infinite panoramic view, enables us to grow without boundaries, and fly free, simple and unfettered in the skies of our individuality.

Be open to live the mystery.

Upon awakening, set aside worries, and behold the symmetric beauty in all of life, right down to the molecule. Existence is magnificent. While our minds create our personal reality, that reality is not *all* reality. Why not peek out of our singular world now and again and behold the living mystery of life with a wondrous eye?

The Point to Remember

Live the mystery!

About the Author

Susan was born in Seattle, WA. Her first profession was a psychotherapist treating those suffering from depression, anxiety, post-traumatic stress, substance abuse, sexual abuse, family violence, and severe mental illness. She employed therapies such as communication skill building, relaxation training, systematic desensitization, bioenergetics, and psychodrama. She has facilitated stress management, parenting, and self-discovery workshops that have aided in the psycho-spiritual healing of many. She has lectured on metaphysical and psychological topics, and been involved in various social activist pursuits.

Her education includes an M.A. in Ed. in Counseling/Human Relations and Behavior (NAU), a B.S. in Sociology (ASU).

Susan writes entertaining books that facilitate personal growth and transformation in a variety genres.

In her words: I love to sing, meditate, and play in nature. I love fairy tales, going outside the box, and reading between the lines. I strive to see what is often missed, and to not miss what can't be seen. There is such a life out there, and in there—beyond all perception! So I close my eyes, feel my inner rhythm, and jump off the cliff of convention. And when I land, though I might be quaking in my boots, I gather my courage and go exploring.

Through travel, study, and work, I've gained a rich awareness of cultural differences among people and their psychosocial struggles. I have discovered that oppression often results from the unexamined adoption of outside perceptions. The healing always has been in the individual's stamina to expel outside perceptions of self and constructively exert one's unique core being into the world. I am driven to facilitate expanded awareness that people may separate who they are from who they are told to be. Embracing personal power by loving our unique selves in our strengths *and* weaknesses . . . forever—is a key to joyous living. My motto is: Trust your story. Live the Mystery.

Acknowledgments

Special thanks to my daughter, Sara C. Roethle, a brilliant writer, who edited this book and helped me design the cover. Thanks to Sarah Nevin Roethle for her excellent proofreading abilities. I also appreciate the loving support of my family and friends. Everyone in our life makes a difference. While we can all stand alone if need be, it is so much more wonderful to stand together.

Made in the USA
Middletown, DE
07 July 2020